Tackling Complex Texts
VOLUME
1

Historical Fiction in Book Clubs

SYNTHESIZING PERSPECTIVES

Units of Study for Teaching Reading, Grades 3–5

Acknowledgments

Sandra Cisneros, in her essay "Eleven," points out that the way you grow old is rather like an onion or like the rings inside a tree trunk or like little wooden dolls that fit one inside the other, each year inside the next one. Her description fits this unit of study. The unit has grown like the tree, the onion, or the little wooden dolls that Cisneros reminds us of. It's grown in those ways as one person, another, and another help us think about yet deeper, richer ways to teach the unit. As the unit has been taught this way and that way, over and over, it's taken on not only new layers and new ideas, but also new contributors.

The primary contributor is Mary Ehrenworth, the coauthor. I'd worked on this book in the series for many months before Mary joined the effort as a coauthor. What a great joy it was to pass the draft to her and to have it returned to me, with more lift to the teaching and more grace and passion and affection for the genre. After that initial collaboration, the book became like a ball that we passed between us, with each exchange adding layers to it. It's fitting that this book, the last in the series, is an ambitious one. Its final volume was written in a whirlwind of intense collaboration, with Mary and I working furiously to try to meet deadlines—deadlines that we kept pushing backward by days, weeks, months as the book overtook more and more of our lives, pulling the entire project off its timetable. I'm grateful to Mary for working side by side with me and for not stinting in her willingness to rethink and revise and reinvent. We wrote four times as many minilessons as you see here now, working tirelessly to make this unit sing. She helped make that happen.

Mary and I absolutely relied upon others to function as readers, critics, field-testers, and sometimes writers, too. Hareem Khan's brilliance is here, especially in the second half of this volume. Julia Mooney helped in a million ways, but especially with the Freedom Fighters' book club. Shannon Rigney Keene helped with the *Out of the Dust* book club.

Many teachers helped with this book, but none gave more time, care, and love to it than Molly Feeney. Molly was one of the original team of teachers who piloted all these units. You will have watched her beautiful minilesson from the second unit, *Following Characters into Meaning*, on the DVD. She taught an early iteration of this unit to her third graders, and researched their reading development across the year and especially within the unit, sharing transcripts of book clubs and conferences with me. Kathleen and I had an open invitation to her classroom, and she and her children shared all their thinking, their reading, and their writing about reading. Molly devoted one entire summer to working as a research colleague in this effort, especially helping us to study student work and to understand children's learning progressions.

This book and the series, too, also owe a great debt to Sarah Colmaire, a fifth-grade teacher who, like Molly, also teaches at PS 199 in Manhattan. Sarah's classroom has been a laboratory for the Teachers College Reading and Writing Project for years.

Sarah has always made us feel utterly welcome to learn from and alongside her students, and she's always been willing to bring her insights and inventions to think tanks and study groups. Sarah is an especially thoughtful reader and writer, and her own literacy enriches her teaching and our community.

Because this unit was revised as many times as it was, the teachers who field-tested all the other units worked with an entirely different draft of this unit. The final volume, then, needed its own round of field work. How grateful we are to Trent DeBerry, who teaches fifth grade at Heathcote Elementary in Scarsdale, to Kelly Boland and Brooke Lipskin at PS 6 in Manhattan, and to Terry McNulty at PS 321 in Brooklyn, for letting us pilot some of these lessons, talk with their historical fiction readers, and gather up their jottings and conversations.

Kathleen is not a coauthor of this book, yet still she worked tirelessly to help with it. The effort to organize and learn from student work was especially demanding in this volume, and Kathleen and I spent many very long days poring over student jottings and transcripts. Kathleen had already given her every ounce of strength to the other books, and her willingness to contribute also to this one was over the top. Rebecca Bellingham worked as a partner during the project of this book, researching two book clubs, transcribing conferences, and especially helping us gather, organize and select student work. Rebecca brought a bright spirit and oodles of talent to this endeavor. Lea Mercantini has earned status as a legend at The Project for her work ethic and commitment to the book lists on our CD.

In earlier acknowledgments, I've thanked most of the Heinemann team. Those thanks pertain also to these volumes. I also want to thank Tina Miller, the firsthand director, for her overall guidance, support, and wisdom. Margaret LaRaia and Kevin Carlson deserve recognition for their tireless, exacting, loving work on the video production piece of the series, which resulted in a terrific DVD. Stephanie Levy worked with endless patience and attentiveness to every detail as the production editor for this series, and we thank her for that. Finally, I'd like to thank Steve Bernier, manufacturing manager extraordinaire, who made sure the books were printed according to our preferences and on schedule—a huge job. These individuals and the rest of the Heinemann team worked tirelessly to get the books out the door and into the world.

Finally, this book is dedicated to the nine school leaders who have especially opened their doors to us, again and again, allowing us to learn alongside their teachers and students. We thank our lucky stars for these educators, each of whom leads a school that demonstrates the best of what is possible in literacy education. None of this would be possible without these leaders.

Contents

"Sometimes we come to places in a story where the action slows down, where there is more description than action. Readers, trust the author. Be loyal, stay side by side, rather than running ahead alone. Probably the author inserted these details so that you could better imagine this place. In good books, readers can trust that we'll learn something important through these descriptive passages."

TACKLING COMPLEX TEXTS — HISTORICAL FICTION IN BOOK CLUBS

VOLUME 2: Interpretation and Critical Reading

PART TWO   INTERPRETING COMPLEX TEXTS

"When we read novels, and specifically when we study texts really closely, we are looking at . . . (I held up a giant question mark) We are looking at . . . something. And here is the thing. No one can tell you, as a reader, what to look at, what to notice, what to think. One reader and another will tend to notice similar things about what is happening in the story—about the plot. But each reader brings his or her own meaning to the story, and to do that, we let different parts reverberate in our lives. Each one of us is the author of our own reading."

"Today I want to remind you that thoughtful readers sometimes press the pause button, lingering to ponder what we've read, and to let a bigger idea begin to grow in our minds. For each reader, there will be passages in a book that seem to be written in bold font, parts that call out to that reader as being important. Often these are passages that harken back to earlier sections in the book and that seem laden with meaning, and we read those passages extra attentively, letting them nudge us to think."

"Readers, you are all writing about big ideas and big questions. And today I want to teach you one incredibly important bit of advice. The writer, Richard Price, has said, 'The bigger the issue, the smaller you write.' He means that when you are writing about big ideas, you lodge your ideas in the smallest details and objects from the story."

"Once readers have paused to think deeply about a book, and developed an idea that seems true, from that point on, readers wear special glasses, special lenses, and look at the upcoming text through those lenses. We read on with our interpretation in mind, and say, 'Ah yes!' or 'Huh? That doesn't fit.' Doing this is one way that we continue to develop our ideas."

Although it is really important to fashion ideas and to care about them, it's also important to be open to new ideas. You don't want to read, or to talk, like you're knees are locked, like you are determined to not let your mind budge even an inch. The reason to talk and to read, both, is to learn. In a good book, as in a good conversation, you can literally feel your thinking being changed."

Contents

Introduction

The Unit in a Nutshell

In Volume 1 of this unit, we teach readers to read complex texts with deep comprehension. With support from a book club, readers will learn to keep track of multiple plotlines, unfamiliar characters, and shifts in time and place. Historical fiction is uniquely challenging in that it requires readers to synthesize text about the evolving setting with text about changing characters who are likely to be vastly different from the readers themselves, and then readers must further synthesize that information with the text of the plot and, usually, with several crucial subplots, all of which often involve unexplained gaps in time and unfamiliar circumstances and consequences. You'll also teach readers how to construct a sense of the setting not just as a physical place but as an emotional place, and in doing so, will help students read with attention to the mood in the text. A town that undergoes war or sudden violence will change rapidly, and readers of historical fiction need to notice ways that changes in setting affect different characters differently. In this unit, we rely on historical fiction to invite readers to work hard to comprehend challenging texts. In doing so, we aim to help students develop a passion for the genre and for history, and we aim to help them develop the imagination to walk in the shoes of characters—and people—whose lives are different from their own.

In Volume 2 of this unit we embark upon the ambitious, intellectual work of interpretation. First within one text, then across texts, and then between texts and their lives, we teach readers to grow nuanced ideas and to read to be changed. As their books become more complicated, readers learn that those ideas are not just about what's happening but also about concepts. They learn not to recite back ideas a teacher gives them, but instead to develop their own ideas, doing the hard, intellectual work that children need to do to grapple with themes. Readers make their ideas more complex as they consider the perspectives of characters whose voices are absent as well as those whose voices are present in texts and as they become not only participants in but also students of an era in history. Readers learn, too, to develop literary language for some of the things they are intuitively seeing in their books, coming to recognize and to use allusions, figurative language, and symbolism to convey ideas that are not easily contained in ordinary language. Although this volume begins as a study in deep comprehension of complex texts and specifically of interpretation, it ends by helping readers appreciate the fact that individuals can take action and make choices that change the world.

SOME HIGHLIGHTED SKILLS

Volume 1: understanding gaps in time and shifts in perspective, reading to learn, synthesizing
Volume 2: interpreting, synthesizing, exploring figurative language and symbolism, exploring themes, writing about reading, reading critically, using personal response

OVERVIEW OF THE UNIT

We chose historical fiction as an essential book club unit for a few reasons. By this time of the year, your students will be ready for more independence, more complicated texts, and more interpretive reading work. Historical fiction will give them opportunities to harness and enhance their reading skills with new and profoundly fascinating challenges. The novels themselves are inherently complex. Inevitably, the characters live in places in which our students have not lived, in times they have not known. The reader must figure out the nature of the setting, the ways people live, and not just who the characters are, but the relationship the characters have to historical tensions. So the reading work will be appropriately intense.

We're also drawn to historical fiction because the stories are often ones of the struggle toward social justice. Whether it is a young girl struggling to assert her independence against the backdrop of the Dust Bowl or two boys struggling to cross the color line during a civil rights movement they don't yet understand, the stories illuminate themes of cruelty and courage, power and resistance. You'll see your children, during this unit of study, realize that reading is, really, about learning how to live.

The unit supports a new social structure—book clubs. When our children leave our care, one of our hopes is that they will have internalized a sense that reading plays an important role in their lives. One of these roles is social. We want them to know the shared pleasure of reading with friends. We want them to know what it's like to come to know someone through the books you read. And we want them to have the experience of building collective interpretations. Long after our students have left our classrooms, one of the ways we'll know that our teaching was effective is that they'll continue to take pleasure in books, they'll be confident in their literary conversations, and they'll have the skills to launch and sustain their own social experiences around texts. You'll see, therefore, that we emphasize a movement toward independence in these clubs. You'll learn how to organize these clubs, how to use your data about readers to fashion particular goals for particular clubs, and how to teach into the structure of clubs as you would teach into guided reading groups or strategy lessons. As part of this, you will teach readers to lift their skills for talking and writing about reading. But most importantly, you'll be coaching your students to self-initiate and to develop the skills they need to sustain their own reading lives.

This unit is organized so that children read in the company of friends, reading shared historical fiction from a particular era with support from a book club. The unit also aims to be sure that the baton is passed to you, as teachers, so that you are able to author your own units of study. To do this, you are especially encouraged to participate in your own adult reading club alongside this unit, giving yourself and your colleagues an insider's perspective on the work you are asking children to do.

The Goals and the Plan for Volume 1: Synthesizing Perspectives

This first volume in the unit teaches readers to read complex texts with deep comprehension, working with support from a book club to keep track of multiple plotlines, many characters, and shifts in time and place.

Teach Readers to Investigate the Special Role of the Setting in Historical Fiction

Your work will begin teaching youngsters to investigate the settings in their novels. Readers who have had a steady diet of realistic fiction often let the settings in their novels fly by them. Picture the setting in *Amber Brown*. It's a school classroom, a bedroom, a kitchen, but none of these settings play especially important roles in the novels. In more complicated texts, though, especially stories in the R/S/T band and above, the setting becomes significant. It may even function as part of the problem that a character has to overcome. It may operate at a symbolic level. The dust of the prairie may mean more than simply that the land is dry.

One of the gorgeous aspects of historical fiction is how it teaches young readers to pay attention to setting. They *have* to figure out when the story is taking place, and where, and what kind of place it is to understand the story at all. So you'll teach your students to be alert for clues about the physical setting and the setting as an emotional space. Is it the kind of town where people are good to each other or where bad things can happen? Is it a place that is on the brink of change or that has been swept up in a war? What is the mood of this place? These will be new questions for your readers. They'll emerge from their study of settings more prepared to tackle the complex shifts in settings in any novel.

Teach Readers to Accumulate and Synthesize Details, Using Reading Tools Such as Timelines and Graphic Organizers

Historical fiction, at the levels at which your children are probably reading, moves swiftly. Readers need to gather a lot of information quickly. In these novels, as in all good novels, details matter. If you learn something on page 2, or in Chapter 1, it's because you're going to need it later in the story. And so you'll teach your readers to accumulate and synthesize details. Essential reading tools such as timelines, graphic organizers, and lists of characters, which your readers may not have needed for a time, now become important tools again. This is important, because one thing you'll be teaching your readers here is that good readers don't wait for a teacher to tell them how to use their comprehension strategies. Strong readers know that as their books get harder, they have to work harder, and they know how to do this. A reading curriculum, like a writing curriculum, spirals. As students move up levels, and into harder books, they'll find they need to consciously harness comprehension strategies. You'll model much of that crucial reading work, so that your students learn to use multiple strategies to make sense of what they are reading. They'll learn to use their pencils as they read. They'll learn to reread on the run, which must become automatic if they are to tackle the kinds of complicated texts that await them. They'll also develop some expectations of the kinds of complications, in terms of time shifts, multiple plotlines, and unfamiliar settings, that await them as they continue to outgrow themselves as readers.

Remind Readers to Bring What They Know of Reading Fiction into Their Work with Historical Fiction

Your students will presumably have come to this, the first bend of the unit, after having spent four to six weeks focusing on reading nonfiction. At the start of the unit, then, you'll need to bring them back to all they learned earlier in the year about reading fiction with engagement and understanding, bringing all they know about envisionment and prediction and about using a knowledge of story structures to help them develop theories about characters. The start of this unit may seem almost as if the teaching cycles backward a bit to reteach some of the earlier work, but in fact, because the characters in their stories are so very different from our readers, this essential reading work is just that—essential. It is harder reading work to imagine the perspectives of characters who live in places and ways that are very different than our own. It is harder reading work to imagine a place that one has never seen and to feel whether a character fits in that place or is unhappy there. And so, even as your minilessons focus on teaching children to work with the invigorating challenges of historical fiction, your mid-workshop teaching and conferences (and some of your minilessons) will support your readers in recalling and utilizing the reading strategies they developed in the first two units of study.

Teach Readers to Empathize with Characters and Notice Their Complexity

Early on in the year, for example, readers learned that at the start of a story, one notices the traits and motivations of the main character, and they empathized with the character. In this unit, you'll help learn about characters not only from their thoughts and actions, but also from their back stories that may (in more challenging texts) be revealed in little bits, throughout the duration of the story. You'll give readers a whole new understanding of the advice you gave them earlier—that it is important to remember that characters are complicated, that they are not just one way. Readers will come to understand that characters may say one thing while thinking something entirely different, and they'll come to see that what one person says about another may reveal as much about the speaker as about the character being described. Readers will understand, too, that characters are emotionally complex, wrestling with problems that are layered and mostly internal and that do not necessarily get solved in a story.

Teach Readers to Construct a Sense of the Setting and to Let this Inform Their Understanding of the Story

But above all, you'll teach readers to construct a sense of the setting in a story as they read and to synthesize this understanding of the setting into their larger understanding of the story as a whole. When readers read texts at the N/O/P/Q band of text difficulty, the settings tend to be places that many readers know—a contemporary classroom or home, for example. The settings tend, also, to be fairly static. Wayside School is described once at the start of the story, but the place itself does not undergo major developments as the plot of the book unfolds. Instead, the setting provides the backdrop. Then, too, in books below levels P/Q, the story could often be transplanted to a different setting without the entire plotline changing. Once readers progress to higher levels of text difficulty, the settings often become less familiar and more dynamic and more essential to the story. This is true not only in historical fiction and fantasy books at these higher levels, but in realistic fiction as well. The rural small town setting in *Because of Winn-Dixie*, for example, is important because one could say that the entire book is the story of how this town changes once Opal and her dog begin to make relationships with a surprising cast of characters. What was once a cold, alienating place becomes a network of relationships—all because of a stray dog named Winn-Dixie and the girl who takes him in. The setting in *Bridge to Terabithia*, too, undergoes major changes. Terabithia itself is a place, and readers need to come to under-stand its evolving traits and its role in the story just as surely as they need to understand the traits of the characters. Terabithia is an adventure, a refuge, a place of sorrow, of terrible endings, and of new beginnings.

Teach Readers to Construct Parallel Timelines

To teach readers to attend to settings in their historical fiction book, you'll teach them that narrative readers construct several parallel timelines as we read—one of the plot and one of the evolving setting. We think about ways in which those two timelines intersect. How do the changes in the setting, in history, affect the story? How do different characters react differently to these changes? Of course, the setting itself needs to be inferred. You'll teach readers, for example, that the transitional passages that tell about daily life—for example, about a character getting from here to there—can't be by-passed because they often reveal a great deal about the world in which the story is set. Readers need to infer all that is implicit from what is given to them. Part of this involves reading with attentiveness not just to the concrete facts of the setting, but to tone and mood and coming to realize that nothing that happens in a story is included acci-dentally. If the lightening flashes and the dark clouds rumble, the impending storm is included in the story for a purpose, and readers profit from thinking, "Why might the author have made it storm just now? What am I supposed to be thinking?"

> *As students move up levels, and into harder books, they'll find they need to consciously harness comprehension strategies.*

Guide Readers Through the Logistics of Reading in Clubs

This portion of the unit, then, asks a lot of readers. They're expected to read more closely, more actively, than ever before. The good news is that readers will not be working alone but will instead be sharing texts with the members of a book club. You'll learn the logistics of clubs—that they meet almost every day at the start of a unit so that club members can forge a social organization that bears their own thumb-prints, that feels more like a real club, a tree fort, than like a reading group.

You'll see the importance of mascots, meeting areas, club rituals, and club goals. You'll see, too, that by giving each club a chance to construct its own identity, you also give yourself a way to help a club tackle a reading project. Those projects will be collaboratively shaped by you and the club members. Based on your assessments of the readers in a club, you steer one club to seize upon the notion that they could do tons of drama, really aiming to act out and experience the books they're reading—and meanwhile helping to develop their fluency. Another club could decide to read more slowly, to do more rereading and more writing about reading. You could help this club develop their ability to read analytically and closely. All club members will need to learn ways to talk and write more thoughtfully and with increasing independence. Fortunately, the books themselves make this work imperative.

The Goals and the Plan for Volume 2: Interpretation and Intertextuality

Teach Children to Develop Multiple Nuanced Ideas About Their Complex Texts

Volume 2 embarks upon the heady intellectual work of interpretation. As the stories your children are reading become more complicated, one of the most important things you'll teach is that their novels are not just about what is happening. The books are not just about the plots. Their novels are about ideas.

Moreover, their books aren't just about one idea. Each book they read will be about more than one idea. This is new work for a lot of readers, especially young readers who came of age searching for a central, or main idea, of a text. In this part of the unit, you'll counteract that limited understanding by teaching your students that reading is about drafting and revising ideas. You'll do this work with your students first within one text and then across texts and then between texts and their lives. You'll teach your readers to grow nuanced ideas and to read to be changed by the new worlds and characters we encounter.

It's crucial to understand that this interpretation unit is not about teaching kids to recite back an idea that a teacher gives them. We will not tell them "the theme" of a book or send them off to seek evidence for an idea they did not develop themselves. You will not skip the hard intellectual work that kids need to do to grapple with intellectual themes. Our goal is that your students learn to articulate significant ideas about their books, that they learn to revise those ideas on their own, and that they learn to reconsider and elaborate on those ideas in the

company of other readers. The book club work will be tremendously important here as your kids learn that our ideas are more powerful in coalition than when we work alone. Indeed, one of the most significant lessons of this unit, and we hope one of the most lasting, will be teaching children that their greatest strength lies in each other.

The interpretation work of this bend begins by teaching students to author their own responses. Too often, in too many places, kids are taught that they don't matter in the curriculum. Not here. Not in your classroom. You'll teach your students that what they bring to texts matters. You'll show them that what they notice in texts is intricately related to their personal and ethical concerns, to the history they bring to the page. You, also, will reveal a history that informs your reading response, showing how you sometimes read as a big sister or sometimes as a victim of bullying or sometimes as an expert on a historical time period. Your students don't need to know this, but you'll be depending on the reading response theories of Louise Rosenblatt. You'll teach that the meaning of a text lies between the book and the reader. It exists in this union. What really matters is that you'll show your kids that *they* matter—that what they bring to reading shapes their understanding.

Teach Readers to Linger in Texts, Noticing Significant Details

That said, you'll also be showing readers how to deepen their understanding and widen the terrain of what they see in novels. You'll show them how some parts of a story seem to be written in bold font. They invite the reader to linger, to ponder. How many of us have first celebrated (and then lamented) the speed at which our children move through books? They're plot junkies. They're reading for what happens. We do it too, of course. We've stayed up late, zooming through a mystery novel or a historical fiction book. We have to know what happens. But books don't reveal their secrets to readers who zoom. And as adult readers, we may zoom, but we still have peripheral vision. We're still alert to significant details, because we're experienced readers. Your students will benefit from being taught to linger in texts.

At first, you'll teach your students that it almost doesn't matter where you pause, as long as you become the kind of reader who does pause. In this lull, before they leap to the next page, you'll teach them to develop initial ideas. You'll teach them to start to ask, "What is this part about?" And then you'll teach them to progress toward asking, "How is this part related to parts that came before? What is it beginning to add up to?" You'll teach them to notice the craft of the story: to mull over objects that appear repeatedly, to be alert to possible symbolism, to notice literary language. Readers learn, too, to develop literary language for some of the things they are intuitively seeing in their books, coming to use allusions, figurative language, and symbolism to convey ideas that are not easily contained in ordinary language.

Teach Readers to Read Critically, Through the Lenses of Perspective and Power

You'll also develop your readers' critical reading skills. One new lens you'll teach will be the lens of perspective. You'll teach your readers to untangle the perspectives in their stories, first by separating the reader's perspective from the main character's (this is hard for young readers, who tend to filter their understanding through their own perspectives) and then by discerning the perspectives of different characters in their novels. A second critical reading lens will be that of power. You'll teach your readers to be alert to power relations in their stories, showing them how critical readers pay attention to who has power, how power is visible, and how it shifts. Finally, you'll illuminate the issue of representation, teaching your readers to ask who counts in their stories, whose perspective is honored, and who may be invisible, marginalized, or stereotyped.

Teach Readers Intertextuality: Reading Between Historical Fiction and Nonfiction to Build Meaning

As your children become adept at interpretation, you'll move toward teaching into intertextuality. All along, your readers, of course, will have been reading in text sets of historical novels. But now you'll teach them to develop their ideas across books, seeing which ideas are true in more than one novel, how some ideas are universal themes that run through many of their books, and how readers begin to assemble text sets and reading projects, either literally or figuratively, by mentally grouping books together. You'll add a strand of nonfiction reading to this work, both so that your readers develop their burgeoning passion for history and so that you show how, when you rub texts up against each other, you ignite new ideas.

Teach Readers that Reading Teaches Us How to Live

At the culmination of this unit, your children should be powerful readers. They should have at their fingertips a ready assemblage of comprehension strategies that will help them tackle, with pleasure, the challenges of increasingly complicated texts. They should be interpretive readers. They should be confident, articulate, and inclusive in their literary conversations. All of this, however, is still not quite enough. We want, here, to do nothing less than to help you show children that reading matters because it teaches us how to live. Books give us insight into lives that we wouldn't otherwise understand. They illuminate issues of social justice. They make visible the dilemmas of history and of the everyday transactions of our lives. They should leave us with lasting lessons, deeper empathy, and mentor role models. At the end of the unit, therefore, you'll bring the lessons students have learned from their books to bear on the urgent social issues that shape their lives. You'll move your students to be affected, no, to be transformed by their books, so that we may all try to live lives of greater courage and integrity. Although this volume begins as a study in deep comprehension of complex texts and specifically of interpretation, it ends by helping readers appreciate the fact that individuals can take action and make choices that change the world.

Tackling Complex Texts in the Company of Friends

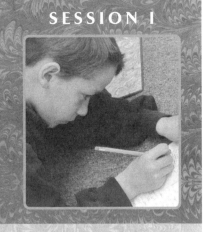

PART ONE

Constructing the Sense of Another Time

IN THIS SESSION,
you will teach your students that readers pay particular attention to details about the setting—what the place feels and looks like and how it changes.

 y this time in your work with these units of study, it is critically important that your teaching is lifting *your* energy, that it is generating passion and purpose and energy in you, so you can pass that energy on to your students. Research is now clear that the single most important element in the teaching of reading is *you*—the teacher. No approach to teaching will ever work if it does not tap an energy source in you.

GETTING READY

- During this unit, you will launch book clubs that will last across the unit. Today, children will read with a cluster of others, not realizing that this grouping will probably become an enduring club. Today, then, will be a day for "stealth" clubs (and a chance for you to tweak your groupings before they become final).

- Using the children's suggestions and your own knowledge of the class, fashion book clubs that, for the most part, each contain four members. The conferring section of today's session provides guidance on putting together those clubs.

- You'll need to make sure that you can provision each of the book clubs for the duration of the units with books relating to a topic or issue, allowing the groups as much choice as you can manage. You'll need to have four copies (or a copy for each member) of each of the books on each topic, for each group for the whole unit. If this unit is five weeks long, each club of readers will read five to ten novels pertaining to one historic time, so provisioning your class with multiple copies of these books is not easy. The *Resources for Teaching Reading* CD-ROM contains leveled book lists of historical fiction that are linked to many different eras. Turn to the conferring section of this session for more about this.

- You'll need to give a picture book to each club, imagining that the club members will take turns reading this book aloud to each other today and will jot and talk in response to it. You'll want the book to convey a sense of place and to imbue that place with atmosphere. We especially suggest you use picture books set in the Holocaust or books set in the era you imagine that club will eventually study.

- Be prepared to recall a historical fiction novel that has swept you away. You may choose to read a paragraph aloud, so choose an especially dramatic moment.

- Choose a short text to read aloud during today's minilesson such as *Rose Blanche*, by Roberto Innocenti. Expect to read the first part of the story today during the minilesson and to finish reading the book outside the reading workshop, during read-aloud time before Session III. You'll want to choose a short text that is related to the historical era of your main chapter book read-aloud, which for us will be *Number the Stars* (but you could select a different read-aloud).

Before launching this unit, think about a historical fiction film or book that you've adored. Perhaps you read *Exodus*, Leon Uris's dramatic novel about the founding of the state of Israel, by flashlight, as I did, imagining yourself living the kind of romantic, dangerous life that Kitty was living. If you have ever been swept up by a historical fiction story, then bring your memories of that story and of that experience to your students. More than that, if you have ever read a book in the company of friends and come to see that book

> *Research is now clear that the single most important element in the teaching of reading is you—the teacher.*

through new eyes because you read it with others, you'll also want to tap into your memories of that experience. Teachers who attend one of the Teachers College Reading and Writing Project's reading institutes never fail to tell us that the opportunity to read and talk about books with colleagues is transformational for them.

One year, my organization received funding to supply multiple copies of books to New York City teachers who wanted to read alongside colleagues. We soon had over 100 groups of teachers meeting in weekly book clubs. Facilitators of those 100 book clubs met with my colleagues and me in a giant think tank, researching the conditions that allowed these groups to thrive and the predictable challenges that threatened to derail them, too. Much of what we

learned through that research has been woven into this unit of study.

The most important lesson that we learned from reading together is that there is reading—and there is *reading*. So often, I am so busy that it is as if I am made of smooth steel. Hurrying here and there, with my cell phone, my email, my appointments, my lists, my roles, my jobs, and my busyness (so proud of my busyness), I can be so busy that nothing really gets through to me. It's as though my life is half lived. The poet, Maxine Kumin, has said, "I am so busy living the life of wife and mother that I don't have time to unfold—it's all in the pleats." Reading—really *reading*—can change that.

This unit of study can be a turning point not only for the kids but also for you and for me. Years from now, when you and I make timelines of our growth in reading, this unit of study can be a star on those timelines.

This session invites—even entices—children into the world of historical fiction and then immerses them in the work readers do right away when reading historical fiction—figuring out where the story is taking place and what kind of place it is. Of course, prior to now readers will have taken note of the settings in books they read, but generally, until now, they may have treated the setting as a bone-dry bit of information. If the story is set in Old Boston in the late 1700s, that's important information for a reader to know, and this unit will return to honor factual information and the process of noting it. For now, though, the session uses short, intense picture books to give readers a felt sense for what it can be like not only to take note of the setting but also to be swept up by it. Readers will hear (and, we hope, feel) that setting is intimately related to atmosphere and mood. You'll urge your students to be alert to the emotional setting as well as the physical setting—to realize that a setting incorporates not just physical details but a sense of how a place feels. They'll come from this session poised to pay extra attention to what the place in a story feels like as well as looks like.

This alertness will especially pay off for readers who are (or who will soon be) reading books in the level R/S/T band of text difficulty or books that are even more complex than those. Think of it: Doesn't it seem that books such as *Freckle Juice, The Wayside School, or Magic Treehouse—books that are in the K/M band of text difficulty—tend to be written with the expectation that the author can simply identify the setting, and then the reader will generate a sense of that setting? The author locates the story in a contemporary school or home, expecting that for most of the books' readers, the reader will simply transplant the story to the school or home that the reader knows best. (Of course, this assumes a reader with a background aligned to the story, and these books will be much more challenging for readers coming from very different contexts.)

In contrast, in more complex books—not just historical fiction but many books in the R/S/T band of text difficulty—readers are asked to hold on to a sense of the setting even as it changes. In these more complex books, the reader's knowledge of the story's setting must develop across the story line because often the change that occurs in the story involves a change in the characters' relationships to the setting. The place itself functions almost as antagonists do, prompting characters to respond. The prairie setting in *Sarah, Plain and Tall evokes great loneliness and nostalgia in Sarah, whose roots are by the sea; in the sequel, *Skylark, it is the unremitting drought that chases Sarah and the children from the land. Because historical fiction tends to start at a time of great historical tension, which almost inevitably means a time of change, readers who pay attention to the feelings that a setting engenders will probably be experiencing rising tension. In most historical fiction, the setting for the story is a place that is in the throes of great pressures. This unit, however, is not simply a unit on reading historical fiction. It is a unit on tackling complex texts. The point of today's session, then, is not simply to entice children to be swept up by the settings in their historical fiction novels. It is to help readers be more attentive to the tone and atmosphere in a setting and more alert to gathering tensions—to the winds of change.

Earlier in this series, I quoted the great poet laureate Lucille Clifton, who spoke at one of the Teachers College Reading and Writing Project's reunions, just as the Rodney King trial had enflamed Los Angeles in riots. "Nurture your imagination," she said. "You cannot create what you cannot imagine." This session aims to nurture children's images of what it can mean to read historical fiction well. By telling them of a time when you were swept up in the power of "Once upon a time, long, long ago . . ." and by using powerful picture books to help them to be similarly drawn into this genre, you use this one session to give your students a big image of the work they'll be doing over the next four to six weeks. You know today's session will in some ways function like the read-aloud of a complex poem: Children will feel what you say and experience what you say, and they will not entirely understand what you say. In the sessions that follow, you'll back up, providing them with pathways and ladders to help them all get aboard this work. But for today, the goal is to tap an energy source in them—and in you.

MINILESSON

Constructing the Sense of Another Time

CONNECTION

Tell a story that shows the way a historical fiction book swept you up and took you to another time and place. Bring that story to life, making your synopsis dramatic.

"Readers, last night I was rooting around in the attic looking for a serving dish I really wanted to use for a dinner I was giving, when I had this amazing experience. It was a little dark and dusty up there. As I was opening and closing boxes, the dust was billowing up, and I began to get that claustrophobic feeling where all you want to do is escape and get out of there. But I really wanted to find that dish. And then, as the dust cleared, I saw, sitting right on top of this one box, an old paperback. Its blue cover was a little torn, there was a tea stain on the binding, and the pages were yellow and wrinkly as if they had gotten wet. It looked as if it had been read a hundred times."

I used my hands to imagine rippling the pages and turning the book over. Then I went on: "The picture on the cover was of a big tanker ship, a rough-looking man with a machine gun, and beautiful woman in a nurse's uniform. The title, in large block letters, said, 'EXODUS.'"

If it's easy to do, you could have the book you are retelling in your hands. But there is something beautiful, as well, about imagining the book and the cover. It lets the children substitute, in their minds, a book that they are as passionate about.

I let my voice get a little low, and even more urgent. "Readers, I saw that title, and I was back on the deck of that ship, with Kitty, the American nurse, and Ari, the Israeli soldier, and all around us, a group of orphans, who were literally starving themselves to death. It is 1946, a year after World War II ended. The children are refugees from the Holocaust—from the death camps the Nazis built to exterminate the Jews and other people they thought unfit. The children on the boat have been taken from their families. They have hidden in attics and basements; they have walked hundreds of miles across icy fields and through dangerous towns. They have hidden from soldiers and dogs. And now, finally, they have almost made it to the Promised Land, the only place in the whole world where Jews will be safe. But when they arrive at Cyprus and are anchored off the rocky shores, the British won't let them land. They are not sure, yet, about the idea of a Jewish homeland, which is where these children are bound.

You'll have your own titles that at some time in your life have swept you away to other places. Exodus was one of the most powerful reading experiences of my young life. And so my voice changes when I think of it, my whole body shows how much I adored reading this book. It's convenient, that as I retold part of this book, I was also able to introduce some of the historical context of our read-aloud, but that was just a lucky chance. The most important thing is to have a book that you have absolutely been entranced by and to show the children what it looks and feels like to get swept away. You could tell a story about being so immersed in a book that you missed the stop on the bus or the subway, or were up half the night, lost in another time, another land, and had been entirely, completely, swept away.

And so the children sit on the boat, in the hot sun. They have been told to go back, but they won't. And now, to convince the British to let them land in peace, they have gone on a hunger strike.

I acted out turning the pages of that book, the story making me sink lower and lower. "Readers, just the front cover of that book whisked me back in time, to the hot deck of that ship. I was Kitty again, terrified for these orphans, and amazed by this rough soldier who was willing to sacrifice them rather than to have them continue to live without a homeland. I had first read this book when I was thirteen. It was my first experience with historical fiction—with stories that are set in other times and places. Until then I never knew that a book could take you so far away, to places where so much was risked, where characters could be so brave, could sacrifice so much, could endure unbearable danger and loss.

I put down the book and let my voice move to a more intimate tone. "As you can imagine, readers, I never got the serving dish. I stayed in the attic, reading, reading, reading. I was caught up, again, in the terrible history of Auschwitz and its aftermath. It was as if, by reading, I could be with Kitty. I could ensure that these orphans would survive.

I sat up straighter then and looked directly at the children, "Readers, when I came down from the attic, I have to tell you that I felt different. I was less concerned with what plates I would use when the company came and more concerned with how I could try to live a life of courage and commitment, as Kitty did. As I fixed supper and got ready for my friends to arrive, I remembered how, when I was a bit older than you and read that book for the first time, it made me want to make a life for myself that added up, that was big and important. As I shredded the lettuce, I thought about you all—and thought that like Kitty, I have found work that lets me do something important. I vowed, too, that I'd try to continue to live with even greater courage and awareness of others, with determination." Then I said, "Thinking about *Exodus* has made me want to immerse myself in this time period, to be swept away from my serving dishes and computer, to imagine myself in those war-torn places, with those incredible characters."

Teachers, you might decide to read aloud a paragraph. Leon Uris is such a dramatic author that it is not hard to choose a part of the text that will draw kids in even more. But keep an eye on the time; we don't want this to make the minilesson too long.

If I had had more time, I would also have told children the truth of that attic story. The truth is that after rereading Exodus, *I realized that I wanted to read lots more historical fiction, and I started with another book by Leon Uris,* Mila 18. *It is about Jewish children who are part of the resistance movement in Poland during World War II.*

Use your experience as a reader of historical fiction to talk up the genre and the unit in general.

"Readers, I can tell that you are getting excited about historical fiction, too, just from listening to these stories. There is something so enthralling about reading stories set in the midst of real historical events. You feel as if you, too, lived in these far away places. You learn what it was like to face threats that we hope we'll never encounter in our lifetime. One thing that we know, just from imagining those orphans sitting on the hot deck of that ship, is that we'll be transported to another time and place. These stories will happen in war zones, in dust storms, in wild and wondrous places that we have never lived in, but we'll *feel* those places through these stories."

Name your teaching point. Specifically, teach children that they need to be ready to pay extra attention to details about the setting in their stories, particularly to what the place feels like as well as looks like, as well as to details suggesting how the place may change.

"Readers, here's the thing: all of us already know what a setting is in a story. It's the place where the story, or scene, happens. But today, I want to teach you that in historical fiction, because the setting will inevitably be unfamiliar to us, we have to really pay attention not just to what the place *looks* like, but what it *feels like*—not just to its physical details but to its emotional atmosphere."

Teaching

Set children up to listen as you read aloud the start of a picture book. Tell them you bring particular expectations because you will be reading historical fiction: You are alert to details of the setting, and you expect trouble will be brewing.

"Today, I want you to get that feeling of being swept away into another time and place by a book. Readers, I've brought a story that I can't wait to read with you, and later you'll have a chance to read other historical fiction picture books. I hope we can use

Teachers, you may be a bit confused when I suggest you talk up the unit—and then I proceed to talk about historical fiction, not about tackling complex texts. The kids will think of this as a unit on historical fiction. You meanwhile know that you are deliberately working with the genre to help your readers develop skills that will be transferable to any genre, and specifically, you are nurturing the skills necessary to read more complex fiction. But as far as the kids are concerned, this is a unit on historical fiction.

You'll notice that I use words like "wild and wondrous," and "war zones and dust storms." This kind of language alerts your children that they are embarking on something exciting.

This teaching point may sound as if it is related specifically to historical fiction, but it's not. If you have a second, go back to the first pages of The Tiger Rising *and reread them with the lens of noticing the emotional atmosphere at the start of that book. You'll see that many of the details at the start of that story absolutely combine to create an emotional atmosphere. This teaching point and most of the content of this book pertains across most complex texts.*

these short, powerful books (with their beautiful pictures) to help us experience historical fiction—and what it means to pay extra attention at the beginning of historical fiction to details that tell us what this place looks and *feels* like.

"We talked during our unit on nonfiction reading about the way that nonfiction readers rev up our minds before embarking on reading a nonfiction text. Before reading any text, it helps to build up our own sense of expectation, and to do so partly by anticipating the kind of experience we're in for. So today and whenever we read historical fiction, we'll want to get ourselves ready to read. I usually remind myself that the story will be set in a time and place that is unlike my own, and I prime myself to be alert to details about what this place is like. Let me tell you one added tip: I also expect that the story will be set in a place where trouble is brewing, so I am also alert for signs that things are changing or that trouble is near. That's the way it usually is in historical fiction.

"This book is called *Rose Blanche*, by Roberto Innocenti. Here's what I know from the blurb on the back cover: This is a story about a girl who lives in a small town in Germany, during World War II. The author says that he wanted to write a story about a place where something terrible is happening, that most people want to ignore. Wow. That's got me fascinated, and a little anxious, already." I opened the book to the first page. "Readers, as I start, I'm revved up to look for details about what kind of place this is—what it looks like and what it feels like.

"Notice that as I read, right from the start I am extra alert to information about what this place is like, and particularly, to any details that suggest change or trouble. Ready?" I showed the first picture. "The story starts with a picture of a small girl wearing a yellow dress and a blue hair bow. She is in a crowded town square, and she and a lot of others are holding small red flags with a black symbol in the middle, a swastika. All around her, soldiers are getting into trucks.

"It says:

> My name is Rose Blanche.
>
> I live in a small town in Germany with narrow streets, old fountains, and tall houses with pigeons on the roofs.
>
> One day the first truck arrived and many men left. They were dressed as soldiers.
>
> Winter was beginning.

Remember that it is common to launch a unit by reading aloud a short text. If you scan the units in Constructing Curriculum, *you'll see that the majority of those units do this. In just a day or two, you can overview the entire experience of what it means to read this new kind of text. Meanwhile, you can support strategies that pertain to the beginning, middle and end of the text, which will help readers choose independent books and quick ones.*

It would be pretty surprising to find historical fiction set in a place where nothing much is happening!

This is a picture book in which the illustrations are done by the author. I've chosen to start with this text because it will provide powerful scaffolding, helping readers to do the work I'm talking about. As I think aloud, I focus on the words of the text rather than the pictures, but the pictures are there, and I show them.

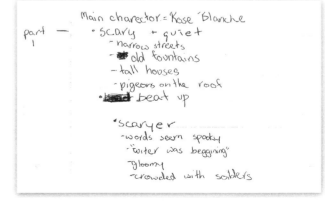

"The children got started doing this, and I moved on then, reminding them to pay attention to the mood of a setting and the revealing details, and urging them to work quickly. With encouragement, a few children sketched rather than wrote about their indelible image. After a bit, I again called for the class's attention. A few of you sketched a picture that stayed with you. Look, here, at this picture Sarah made when she finished *The Lily Cupboard*, a picture book about a small Jewish girl named Miriam, who is hidden in a cupboard when the German soldiers come. Sarah had written that she would never forget how Miriam tried to comfort this rabbit she was taking care of, even as she shivered in fear in the cupboard. So then she quickly sketched a rabbit, with Miriam's two hands holding it with love. Isn't that lovely?" I showed her work to the class. *[Fig. I-8]*

"So, readers, when you finish a book, one way to hold the story in your hearts longer, perhaps forever, is to think about the images that stay with you—the indelible pictures you see in your mind. Then you can write, sketch, or talk about why those images are important. This will be a way to imprint the story, forever, on your mind. Some of you may want to continue working on capturing your indelible images when you are at home tonight." The next day, Danny brought in a sketch he'd made from *Rose Blanche*, and some writing about the sketch. *[Figs. I-9 and I-10]*

Showing a variety of responses, both written and sketched, is a wonderful way to honor children's strengths and also a way to celebrate their independence with this unit. The children themselves decided how they wanted to shape their responses, which makes them that much more powerful.

Figure I-8

Figure I-9
Danny captures an image from *Rose Blanche*.

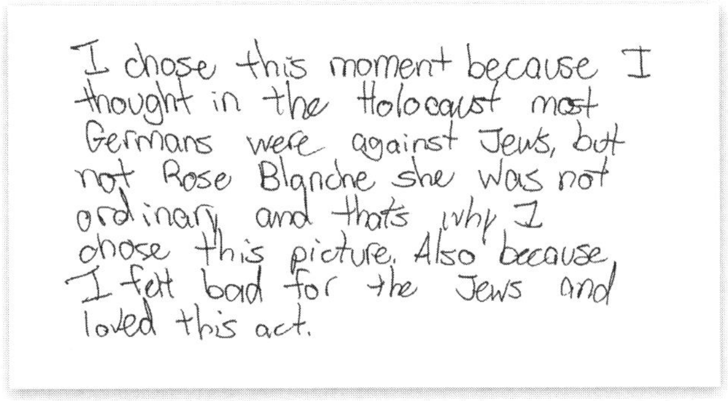

Figure I-10
Danny tries to explain why the one image he'd selected captures *Rose Blanche*.

Formative Assessments to Guide Unit Planning

In the assessment interludes prior to now, I've described some of the formative assessment work that my colleagues and I did as we wrote, piloted, and revised these units of study. Now, for this final unit of study, I want to address instead the assessment work that I hope *you* do as you and your colleagues prepare to teach using these books.

Decide If This Unit Is Right for Your Students This Year

For starters, you need to draw on your assessments of your own students to be sure that you're making a wise decision to teach this unit, at this time, with your class. Remember, the books in this series are not meant as a script for your teaching but as a description of our teaching and a resource for you as you invent your teaching.

If You Decide to Postpone This Unit

Since the first time I wrote the units, in a very sketchy draft, almost a decade ago, third-grade teachers have decided fairly often to either forego a unit of study on historical fiction altogether or to teach it later in the year, when their students are more ready for it, opting instead to teach mystery or humorous books (or something else) for now. It also works strategically if some teachers in a school decide to postpone the unit on historical fiction because this means that text sets of multiple copies of books don't need to be dispersed among all the classrooms at the same time. Of course, if some teachers—let's imagine this as the third-grade teachers—decide to postpone this unit, those of you who make this decision will need to think about the unit you'll teach in its place. In *Constructing Curriculum*, we've provided more support for some units than others, and you may opt for one of the units around which we've provided more rather than less support simply because

you may still want that support. Your children would probably do just fine even with another unit on character—as long as the unit includes different minilessons and is built around a different read-aloud! On the other hand, you may decide to teach a book club unit, and perhaps you'll do so around mystery books. This would be challenging for you because you'd need to develop your minilessons, but this is a tried-and-true all-time favorite unit for students, and the chances that it'll work well for you are high. The unit on humor is newer—you may want to pioneer it!

If You Decide to Teach This Unit with Your Students, Tweak It Based on Whether It Is the Fourth or the Sixth Unit in Your Year

Before you launch into the unit, you will want to read the introductory descriptions for both volumes just to be sure that you want to teach this unit following the general pathway that Mary Ehrenworth and I followed in our teaching.

As you preview the unit, you'll notice that in this unit, as in others, the bends in the road are somewhat separate. The first bend supports strong comprehension of more complex books, and the final two bends, taken together, support interpretation and critical reading. You won't want to teach the second two bends without teaching the foundational one.

On the other hand, if you teach younger readers or readers who you believe will need a lot of help with the content of Volume 1, you could decide to make Volume 1 into your entire unit, using some of the small-group work and conferring work as minilessons, and inventing other minilessons in response to struggles you see children experiencing. In the extensions on the *Resources for Teaching Reading* CD-ROM, you'll see another complete historical fiction unit, and you may adapt minilessons from that unit for yours. Then, too, you can definitely review the teaching you have already done earlier in the year, selecting minilessons, mid-workshop teaching points, small-group work, and the like to reteach. For example, you could reteach some of the strategies from *Following Characters into Meaning*, now teaching them within the context of historical fiction. As another example, if your assessments tell you that your readers need a second round of instruction on keeping their reading logs as scientists might, collecting and studying accurate data, then you could look back on previous teaching you did to support that work, look at what your students are and are not doing, and then adapt, tailor, and rewrite the previous teaching to fit this new context, or invent new teaching altogether.

You'll see that in this unit we bring readers into book clubs, usually containing four readers, and channel those clubs to read multiple copies of books from within the historical era (e.g., Civil War) that the club selects. To teach this way, using book clubs, you'll need multiple copies (usually four) of historical fiction books at levels your children can read. Assess your library and your school's book room and budget to determine if this is doable. If not, tailor the plan to your situation. For example, if you do not have four copies of books, do you have sufficient numbers of duplicates so that you can support children working in same-book partnerships, instead of clubs? If so, perhaps members of a partnership can read copies of the same book, progressing in sync through it, perhaps later swapping books with another partnership that might be reading books set in the same era (and perhaps in this way children will be able to sometimes talk as a foursome). Do you have enough books if children only read the multiple copies of historical fiction books when they are in school, reading other books (independent historical fiction or related nonfiction) at home?

Anticipate that Children Will Progress Along a Trajectory of Skills

As you mull over the plans for your unit, I urge you to keep in mind that when you teach reading, as when you teach writing, you won't teach one particular skill until all readers have "mastered" it. Remember to think of skill development as having a trajectory, a learning pathway, and to teach so that all your readers progress along that trajectory.

Expect that your teaching should be powerful enough that individual readers will be able to see themselves progress along the trajectory of a skill in noticeable ways. But you needn't expect that there will come a time when you say, "Okay, all my readers have mastered inference"— (or determining importance or critical reading or any other aspect of reading). So you also needn't persevere teaching the same skill on and on and on until everyone "gets it." This curriculum is a spiral curriculum for a reason: readers need to always work on an orchestration of multiple skills. Their development of one skill is reliant on their parallel development of other skills. Then, too, mastery is not the goal, because in fact, none of us have mastered the skills of proficient reading. Every reader continues to develop our reading skills, especially when we try a new genre or a text that is a bit hard for us. I work hard to envision when I am reading the directions to fix my computer! Just as no writer will ever say, "I've mastered writing with voice," or "I'm done working on developing characters," so, too, no reader will master the skills you are teaching in reading.

Create an Informal Formative Assessment Tool

As you plan for your upcoming unit, I can't emphasize enough how valuable it will be if you take the time to do some informal formative assessments. When Mary and I finished a draft of this unit (long after our team of pilot teachers had taught the initial draft of it), I gave a copy of it to a think tank of fourth- and fifth-grade teachers. We suggested that before embarking on the unit, these teachers conduct the formative assessment that I'll describe to you here. Then we helped those teachers (and others who also did this formative assessment) learn from their students' work and, when relevant, tweak plans for the unit, right from the start.

To conduct this assessment, teachers located multiple copies of two brief historical fiction books, on a level N book and on a level R book (that is, one representing the start of each of the two bands of text difficulty in which most of the teachers' readers were working). Then, they embedded a dozen or so free-response questions into those texts in places where most proficient readers would be apt to do a particular kind of mental work. We developed a set of such questions for *Animal Adventures*, one of the books in the *Little House* series, adapted from

Laura Ingalls Wilder's *Little House* books, and one set of questions for Patricia MacLachlan's sequel to *Sarah, Plain and Tall,* entitled *Skylark.* The tool we developed for *Skylark,* and a description of ways we've used it to inform unit planning, follows.

A Possible Text Level R Assessment

To understand this assessment, it helps to know a bit about the book involved. *Skylark* is the continued story of Jacob, Sarah, Caleb, and Anna's journey to come together as a family when the conditions of the land threaten to separate them. At the start of the book, Sarah and Jacob are newly married, and the family is happy. Then it stops raining. A drought makes the days so hot and dry that the leaves fall to dust on the ground. When their wells dry up, neighbors begin to leave. Jacob, however, remains optimistic. This has happened before; they'll survive it now. He says they will never leave the prairie; their names are written in the land. But the children, Anna and Caleb, fear that Sarah will return to her native Maine, where it is cool and green, and rainstorms are plentiful. Sarah says she won't leave, but her ambivalence about this is ever-present and, finally, grows as the situation becomes more bleak. When grass fires begin, and the barn burns down, Jacob tells Sarah that she and the children must go to Maine. There isn't enough water for all of them to live on the prairie anymore. He will tend the animals and the house. Sarah takes the children to Maine while Jacob stays. Weeks go by. Maine is beautiful, but Sarah and the children miss Jacob. Then one day Jacob arrives in Maine and announces that it has rained at last at home. Reunited, with a new baby on the way, the family returns to the prairie.

This informal assessment tool is exactly the same as the ones we've described earlier in previous assessment sections. As in those instances, we selected two different books, at different levels, so that readers would work in texts that their running records suggested would be within grasp (or easy) for them. The questions we embedded in *Skylark* were as follows:

- On p. 3, after the second paragraph:

  1A. What do you know about Sarah? How do you know?

  1B. If you haven't already done so, read the blurb and look at the cover.

What more do you now know about Sarah?

- On p. 7, after the sentence: *"I'm writing Sarah's name in the land, he said,"* (toward the bottom of the page):

  2. Why is Caleb writing Sarah's name in the dirt?

- At the bottom of p. 9:

  3. At this point in this story, what seems important about the prairie, where they live?

- At the page break on p. 11:

  4. Why is Sarah staring and smiling at Seal, the cat?

- At the break on p. 25:

  5A. What do you think this letter makes Sarah feel?

  5B. What do you think this letter makes Anna (the person telling the story) feel?

- At the bottom of p. 32:

  6. What does Anna think as she watches the neighbors, Joseph and Caroline, pack up and leave?

- After the second paragraph on p. 43:

  7A. What do you think will happen in the rest of the story?

  7B. What makes you think that?

- At the page break on p. 50:

  8A. How does Sarah feel right now?

  8B. Is that the only way she feels?

- On p. 62, at the end of paragraph one:

  9. Where are they going?

- At the bottom of p. 68:

  10. What is the author really, really saying here?

- At the end of the book:

  11. What is this whole story really about?

The teachers with whom we were working did not want to devote a lot of class time to this assessment, so they gave this to their youngsters as homework for a weekend, letting students know their work would not be graded (and asking that they not recruit others to help with it) and that this assignment, like their reading logs, would give them a chance to study themselves—this time as readers of historical fiction. The teachers explained the concept of baseline data, helping readers to feel part of this study of their own habits and ways as readers.

Some Practicalities in Conducting This Assessment

Be absolutely sure that *you* read the books that you ask your children to read. I flew through *Skylark* the first time I did this, just to get the gist of the story line and was flabbergasted when I reread the book to see how much *I* had missed. I encourage you to sit up, pen in hand, be alert, and read the book in a way that lets you take in the details of it. It is brief. In an hour of reading, you can mentally "own" the book so that when you read a child's response to it, you won't need to think, "Did the book say that?" Unless your own sense of the book is firm, you'll find you don't have a standard for reflecting on your children's reconstructions of the book.

As we've described earlier, your children will read the book, and when they come to the spot you've marked by a Post-it, or otherwise designated, they'll write a response to the question you've written for that spot. Sometimes, teachers prepared one question on the visible Post-it, and after the child had answered that one question, there would be a second Post-it, underneath it, asking a follow-up question. In some instances, it was too complicated to make little piles of Post-its and distribute these throughout the pages of the books, in which case, at the start of this work, we walked a group of children through the book, showing them where to put a Post-it or two, each with a number on it, and those numbers then sent them to a sheet with questions and spaces to answer each.

In any case, after you've collected your children's responses, I suggest you get yourself a cup of coffee and settle down to simply read through them all, letting yourself take in the whole landscape of their responses before you figure out how you want to study these in more depth. You may want to have made a few copies of the responses so that you can shuffle them into different sorts of configurations. (If your children responded on the computer, you'll save trees and time, although you may find yourself as old-fashioned as I am, preferring to sort hard copies into piles and files.)

What You May Notice First: Surprise Strugglers

You will probably notice that some children who you've assessed at this level through running records (where the assessment tool is a 250-word passage) seem over their heads when working with a book-length text at this level. You definitely do not want children to habituate a sort of reading that leads them to take a rich, complex level R text like *Skylark* and glean from it a text that is vastly simpler, less nuanced, like a poorly written level M text!

So, you'll want to start the unit by thinking about what you want to do with these readers. Do you want to try keeping them reading at the text level that running records suggested they can handle, with you moving heaven and earth to help them derive a richer and more detailed understanding of the story? If so, you will definitely want to come right out and tell these readers what you have noticed, perhaps even telling their parents as well, so as to rally all hands on deck toward working to help them see more, think more, and notice more in the texts they will be reading during the upcoming unit.

These readers will benefit enormously from you (or someone) rereading the first chapter or two of whatever book they are reading aloud to them and their club mates aloud so they can notice how much they missed during their initial reading of it and also construct a firm sense of the book, using this as the foundation as they read onward. You may suggest that if possible, parents reread a chapter or even just a bit of a chapter to the child often, talking about the details of that chapter and about how the chapter on hand connects back to earlier chapters (perhaps even to the preceding bit that the parent had read earlier).

Then again, you might decide that the best plan is to direct your readers to easier texts, while also doing a variation of all that I've described so far to help readers develop a felt sense for a much more active, constructive, and grounded sort of reading experience.

Of course, instead of reading aloud to support comprehension, you can draw on other methods. For example, to help your students construct fuller, closer understandings of texts, you may want to give text introductions for many of the books that your children read in their book clubs—and actually you can even give text introduction to turning-point chapters or to portions of a book. Of course, this means getting to know those books yourself, but you'll find that the reading is a joy, and that once you have four or more readers working with one text, it's possible for you to know many of the books that your class is reading. This knowledge will help your teaching feel more grounded.

A Closer Examination of Students' Reading Work: Finding Strengths

In any case, after the initial feeling of, "Wow, they are missing so much that I expected them to be noticing," you'll want to look more closely at your students' reading to ascertain whatever you can about the work that they can do well and the work they may need support to do.

For example, the study group of teachers with whom I worked noticed that most of their students seemed very able to rely on a knowledge of story structure to think about *Skylark*. When the question was asked, "What do you think will happen in the rest of the story?" even readers who struggled with some other questions were able to use their knowledge of how stories usually go to help them predict. Kayla wrote, "I think at the end of the story something good might happen like they will have enough money to move somewhere cool or like it might rain. There might be stuff for them to eat . . . if it rains, the crops will grow big and they can eat a bigger meal." When asked, "What makes you think that?" she answered, "Because usually at the end of every story I've read, it's always a happy ending and what the characters wished for. Let's say that in one story a person needed money—at the end, they will get money."

Ewan answered the question "What do you think will happen in the rest of the story?" by writing, "Well. I think they are probably going to find water, because that seems like the problem in the story and usually there is a resolution." When he was nudged to account for his prediction, he said, "From past books I've read, there's a problem and a resolution. I haven't read that much in this book yet and I think the problem will get worse, and then there's a turning and then there's a solution. I think it will rain in the end."

In a similar way, these teachers found that many of their students could articulate theories about the characters using precise language and citing text references.

You will need to look across your own students' responses, of course, but there's a fair chance that some of what we've found, you will find, too.

Are Children Understanding the Importance of Story Elements?

As you examine what your children tend to be able to do easily, without support from you, you'll be learning not only about them but also about your own teaching. And as you notice what a far number struggle with, this, too, will nudge you to reflect on (and to extend) your teaching. You'll probably want to notice your children's understanding of perspective, setting, characters, and theme.

NARRATOR

This study group of teachers was surprised to find that a fair percentage of their students read several chapters in the story without discerning who the narrator was. (In *Skylark*—as in *Sarah, Plain and Tall*—the narrator is young Anna.) When one question asked, "What do you think this letter makes Anna, the person telling this story, feel?" Ewan answered, "Oh, I thought Sarah was telling the story. Oh, okay, I think she feels the same." The teacher's surprise was not only that this perspective was confusing to readers, but also that the children seemed to have accepted this amount of confusion, of dislocation, and continued to read, not alarmed by it and therefore not rereading to determine the narrator!

Certainly this, then, became something the teachers resolved to address early on during an early minilesson in the unit. The teaching point they fashioned was this: "Before getting too far along in our reading, readers check and do work to make sure we know who the narrator is." (Keep in mind that the goal of this teaching was not to help children realize that the narrator of *Skylark* is Anna! That kind of teaching only works for the one particular text.) Working together, the teachers decided when the new minilesson would need to come in the unit and talked about whether this could be taught using the existing read-aloud text or whether they'd want to reference a familiar picture book.

SETTING

The teachers were not entirely surprised to see the number of students who read *Skylark*, in which the prairie figures strongly, without grasping what or where the prairie is. Some children saw mention of a barn and thus brought the image of a New England farmyard to their experience of the book. Some, when asked what was important about the prairie, asked, "What's a prairie?" as if the term was entirely new, even though it figures predominantly in the text. One reader whose ideas about people in the book were astonishingly nuanced and complex had absolutely no sense of Maine, of the prairie, or of anything pertaining to the setting. Again, this nudged teachers to be sure their teaching would highlight the importance of accumulating knowledge about the story's setting.

Are Children Working with a Deep, All-Encompassing Sense of the Characters?

On the other hand, some readers were keenly interested in the geography and history of the book and yet did not think about the characters with complexity. When asked about whether Sarah might go to Maine, for example, more than one child responded as if the question were a silly one. "Of course not, she said more than once she wasn't going!" Anyone who knows this book or its prequel knows that Sarah's wish for her home in Maine is a central dynamic in the story. Teachers, seeing this, realized that just as some of their small-group work would need to help readers who tend to focus on characters to also attend to setting, so, too, other small groups would need to help readers who naturally notice setting, geography, and history develop more complex understandings of character.

But the most striking thing for these teachers was the fact that time and again, when asked how a character might be feeling during particularly poignant passages in the text, a fair number of readers seemed to only name the most superficial, obvious, plot-driven aspects of the story. For example, early in the story, just after Papa and Sarah have gotten married, there is talk of how Seal, Sarah's cat, is gaining weight. She's pregnant with a litter of kittens. Papa asks if she has ever had babies before and watches Sarah's face closely as she says that, no, this is her first pregnancy. Sarah stares at Seal for a long time, and Papa stares at her, watching her closely. Her face breaks into a smile. "Kittens!" she says. "Kittens!" When asked why Sarah might be staring and smiling at Seal, not one child conjectured that this might have something to do with newly wed Sarah's own wish to have a child (which is, in fact, how the story ends). When asked, "Why is Sarah smiling at Seal, the cat?" Omar answered, "Because the cat is gonna have kittens." The prompt, "Can you tell me more?" yielded nothing.

Kayla's answer was similar. "Because she likes kittens." Only Kayla elaborated more, saying, "Maybe she just likes kittens. Maybe she really, really, really likes kittens because they are so cute and furry and she has always had one."

Ewan suggested, "Sarah is smiling at the cat because she never had one and she wants to get a good look to make sure if they needed to find it, they could remember what the cat looks like."

Of course, perhaps it would have required a more adult perspective for young readers to infer that Sarah, too, wanted to be pregnant, but this was just one of many signs that readers needed help with interpretation, which is, after all, exactly what the unit aims to provide. That is, although the children's surface-level interpretations of the incident involving the cat are only one instance and could be discounted, as we continued to study their responses, it became clear that many children had very literal understandings of the text in general. For example, at one point, when neighbor after neighbor has moved away, and when Sarah is tempted to do the same, she watches her best friends pack up all their worldly possessions and move away as well. When asked what Sarah feels as she watches her friends and neighbors pack up and move from the prairie, leaving clouds of dust behind them, many children produced answers that would have been equally true for anyone watching a friend move.

Chase wrote, "I think she might be sad because her friend is moving. Maybe they are best friends and you don't want them to leave."

Juan wrote, "She is shocked because she said you can't just leave. She is mad because they are leaving."

Dylan wrote, "She is upset. She feels bad they are moving. Caleb says they are not going to come back."

Are Children Drawing on the Whole Text As They Interpret?

Quite a few readers answered the question of how Anna is feeling as she watches her neighbors move in a manner that took into account only that single page in the text. Instead of pointing out the other neighbors who had already gone, and the worry that Sarah, too, might go, these readers talked about this incident as if it were a freestanding one, existing in isolation from the rest of the text. Contrast this with Marissa, who wrote a detailed answer that went on and on, containing within it, "She doesn't want them to leave because there weren't a lot of people to begin with and she wants them to pitch in and make things better so they get enough food for another week or so. A whole cycle of things are happening. One person leaves, then a whole bunch leaves. Everybody is getting sad because of the leaving and the drought and no water and it doesn't look as pretty as before, and at the beginning, there were lots of fires so they will be happy to leave because it is getting dangerous."

Interestingly, the responses are not different when a coyote circles the house looking for water and Sarah intercedes as the father raises his gun to shoot the parched animal. To Sarah, this animal is one more sign of the devastation in the prairie, reeling from the drought, and one more ominous note pushing her to leave Papa and the prairie. But to many readers, the coyote was just a coyote.

Then, too, when Sarah, who is surrounded by the bone-dry prairie receives a letter from her family in Maine, which tells about the lushness of Maine, mentioning that Sarah's sister's hat flew off into the sea, and the reader is asked, "How does Sarah feel, reading this letter?" Omar's answer was merely, "Kind of bad for her aunt because she'll miss her hat." When asked, "How does Anna feel (referring to the ten-year-old narrator who clearly is worried that Sarah will return to her home of origin), Omar asked if he could look back at the text, and after rereading it carefully, he replied, "I can't find the answer."

Respond to the Patterns in Children's Responses Through Unit Planning

Children's responses created a tremendous amount of excitement in the teachers who were planning to adapt the unit that Mary and I taught so that it would support their youngsters.

Moving Children Toward Deeper Interpretation

You will need to figure out your own way to tailor this unit toward the needs of your children, of course. The adapting teachers were thrilled with the emphasis on interpretation in the unit but also wanted to do more work with the children after the first volume to ready them for the second volume. For a long while, they wrestled with how they could begin to move children toward more interpretive stances even before the unit began devoting itself to this in Volume 2.

Synthesis

They decided to emphasize synthesis, helping readers know that when one reads one part of a text deeply, this means by definition bringing other parts to bear. They wrote a minilesson in which they asked students, "What if I gave you a ticket to a big event?" Then they said, "Think about reaching out, holding that ticket in your hands, and think about what thoughts would cross your mind. My hunch is you wouldn't think only about this small, rectangle of red paper in your hand. My hunch is you'd remember other tickets you've held, events that you attended. Maybe you would remember a particular event you went to, at a stadium or in a theater. Maybe you'd remember someone else who has gone to a big event lately. My point is, holding the one ticket, your mind would leap backward to earlier events—and would leap forwards, too, to possibilities. You wouldn't just consider the little scrap in your fingers. You'd consider what it has meant and what it might mean."

The teachers' point was that one way to help readers think more inferentially involves helping readers draw on earlier parts of a book, earlier pages, when responding to a question. They decided that the students who made strong answers to the question "What does Anna think as she watches the neighbors pack up and leave?" didn't invent that response out of thin air. Instead, they drew on what they knew from earlier in the text and from life.

Interpretation

Finally, the teachers decided that their students absolutely needed them to plan to spend extra time and instruction working with interpretation. Many children responded to the question "What's this book really, *really* about? What are the big ideas of this book?" with a retelling. They did not seem to have an image that some other kind of thinking might be called for in that question. The teachers suspected this was a deeper issue than a misunderstanding of the question.

Omar answered, "It's about a family that had no mother and they got a mother. They were poor but not so poor. One day they ran out of water so they went to Sarah's house where Sarah used to live. They started to be happy. It rained and they were so happy. Then Anna wrote a letter to her dad but didn't say it rained. At the end they saw their dad with the barn and their pets. That's it."

Children's miscues are always fascinating—and this was the case even when their miscues didn't revolve around accuracy as they read a text aloud but instead, around their instinct to retell when asked to interpret. How much this thinking revealed! Even the readers who relied on retellings sometimes brought their own spins to the story.

Victoria, a lover of animals, answered the question "What is this whole story really about?" in a way that suggested that she sees the world through the lens of her own interest in animals. She said, "The story is about this boy and girl, they live on this house on a prairie and their mother died so Sarah marries their father, so part of the prairie burned so Caleb and Anna needed to go to Maine with Sarah and her cat Seal. The dad wanted to stay to take care of Nick and Lottie, the dogs, and Seal, Sarah's cat, who couldn't come because she was having babies—four of them, three gray and one orange because Seal, the cat, married (well, kind of married) the orange cat who used to live next door. Now the dad comes to Maine to visit them and he says it is all right and you can come home and the animals were all there." Victoria is not the only reader who applies her own lens to the text, but hers was one of the most entertaining! Even before the unit began, the teachers who conducted this assessment had tons of notes about conferences they might want to give to kids.

Of course, some readers did try to draw forth a life lesson from the text, but many seemed to be uncomfortable doing so. When trying to talk about Big Ideas, many sounded like Hallmark greeting cards. One wrote, "I think *Skylark* is about always believing and that you have to trust your beliefs and then what you believe will come true. Sarah and Caleb and Papa and Anna really wanted it to rain and believed it would rain and it came true."

Another reader suggested the text was about "how miracles happen. Like a lot of things happened that weren't supposed to happen. There are miracles in the world like when it rained in the book at the end." Or, the book is about "the love between Jacob and Sarah and the family." All of these readers seemed like they were talking and thinking in a whole new genre—making the unit's emphasis on interpretation seem all the more important—and challenging, too.

Of course, others found this easier. Ewan suggested the book tells us, "It's hard to move away from your family members that you've been with a long time."

Lena revealed a lot about her prior instruction when she wrote, "What she's saying up top is that now that the dad is gone, they're all sad, but what's tucked under the skin is, everything isn't perfect and sometimes you have to leave someone you love and it's hard. The whole story is about . . . right now I'm leaning toward how something so small like rain can affect multiple people's lives really deep and hard. It causes a move, and the separation of a family."

As you and your colleagues think about the work that your students do when reading a historical fiction book and responding to questions you insert into that text, you'll find yourself reminded that this unit is not really about a particular genre at all. It is about teaching kids to read. The books and the unit provide the opportunity. The door is wide open.

Collaborating to Comprehend Complex Texts

I cannot stress enough how important it is for you and your colleagues to participate in this unit as insiders by giving yourselves even just a little bit of time to read historical fiction in the company of colleagues. Try it. Order enough copies of *Number the Stars* (or any other book you select as the touchstone for this unit) so that you can read ahead of the kids with your colleagues. If you prefer, read an adult historical fiction book. Above all, set aside time to meet in your own adult versions of book clubs. You'll come to know not only the books and the read-

GETTING READY

- During the minilesson, you will launch book clubs that will last across the unit. You'll want children who read together yesterday to sit near each other, because eventually it will emerge that these are the clubs that will last across this unit. Perhaps distribute the books they read yesterday across the meeting area before you convene the class and ask children to sit near the book they read.

- If you anticipate any unhappiness on the part of some children that have been put with readers with whom they would rather not work, plan to have strategic conversations, saying, "I've been thinking about you, and I want to show you some work I think the four of you are ready for. . . ." This can wash away potential disruption.

- At the heart of this minilesson, you'll interview two children to learn about the interesting things they have done with clubs outside school. Select kids who seem really connected to an activity—ideally, to an activity that interests others. Interview these children about their clubs beforehand so you can steer the questions you ask during the minilesson in ways that elicit the sorts of details that will apply to book clubs. That is, if one child's scout troop goes on trips every weekend, steer clear of that detail. But if that child's troop has a ritual for how it starts every club meeting, that detail would be a great one to elicit.

- Consider what materials you could provide to help club members turn a group into a club. You'll probably encourage them to have a club folder, and you may also suggest large sheets of poster board for a club logo and motto, suggesting that later the club members convene around this poster board as if it were a table.

- Prepare a chart entitled "Creating a Constitution for Our Club" for use during active involvement. You may print individual copies from the *Resources for Teaching Reading* CD-ROM.

- You will have already helped some of your clubs select a historical era, and today you'll launch the rest of your clubs. You'll want historical era–based baskets of books that are roughly equivalent in text difficulty, such as a basketful of R/S/T books on the Depression and another of K/L/M books on the Civil War.

ing processes each of you uses, but also each other so much more deeply because of the shared journey you take together.

Book clubs are the perfect venue for you to experience the extraordinary power that can come when you teach from the position of an insider, of a person who has experienced what you are asking children to experience. Gandhi was wise when he said, "You must be the change you wish to see in the world." This unit can allow you and your kids, to

> *You will see yourself differently, and see others differently, because of what you read and how you talk about that reading.*

tap into the social power that is available when people read within reading communities, and the unit can also help you and your kids learn the power of deep, interpretive comprehension. This unit will not only allow you and your colleagues to read some of the most enthralling books on your shelves; it will also give you a venue for thinking, "How can I live differently because I've read this book?" You will see yourself differently, and see others differently, because of what you read and how you talk about that reading.

In a school where reading instruction is alive and vital for kids, teachers too will be readers. When I work with principals, we sometimes remind them that when they step back to assess the teaching of reading in their schools, they need to ask not only whether *kids* are progressing from one level of complexity to another but also whether *teachers'* energy for teaching is going up. More specifically, I think it is important to ask, "When this teacher (and that one) talks about her teaching decisions, do those decisions come from the fire of her own life experiences? Does she draw on her own experiences as a reader when she talks and thinks about her teaching of reading and writing—and does this give her teaching intimacy and weight?"

This unit of study can be a turning point not only for the kids but also for you. Years from now, when you make timelines of your growth in reading, this unit of study can be a star on those timelines. It can be monumental to you if you approach the unit thinking, "I'm going to gather my courage and take my own reading deeply seriously. I'm going to try to outgrow myself as a reader. And I'm going to do that within a reading club comprised of colleagues—and of my students."

"As any new innovation unfolds," Michael Fullan, the author of a score of books on school reform, writes, "leaders must pay close attention to whether they are generating passion, purpose, and energy—intrinsic motivation. Failure to do so is a surefire indicator that the innovation will fail." If you make the choice to experience this unit from the inside, then there is no doubt in my mind but that the reading workshop will indeed generate intrinsic motivation: passion, purpose, and energy.

# MINILESSON

Collaborating to Comprehend Complex Texts

CONNECTION

Suggest that just as fantasy books take children to powerful new worlds, historical fiction books can do the same, only these worlds will be real worlds that existed in the past.

"Readers, we talked earlier this year about how the children in C. S. Lewis's *The Lion, the Witch and the Wardrobe* were sent to the country to stay with a professor during the war, and when they were playing hide-and-seek in his rambling country home, Lucy decided to hide in the far corner of a closet—a 'wardrobe.' She pushed her way past furry coats, deeper and deeper into the closet. Instead of coming to a wall at the back of the closet, she suddenly found herself standing in snow. A tree bough brushed against her arm, cold and wet. Ahead she saw a lamp gleaming in the woods. Soon she met an amazing creature: kind Mr. Tumnus the faun, a man with goat legs.

"During this upcoming unit of study, we'll enter books, like Lucy entered that closet, and we'll find ourselves standing in new worlds. But those worlds won't be the imaginary worlds of Narnia or Middle Earth; instead, the worlds will be real ones that existed long ago. We may wake to find soldiers and tanks driving through the town we live in, as Rose Blanche did, or we may find wild winds sweeping our farm away and endangering our family. We may find ourselves hiding in boxcars to escape soldiers who want to kill us or falling asleep curled under the bow of a clipper ship as it sails the Atlantic Ocean.

"We'll be reading historical fiction, and we know already, from reading *Rose Blanche*, that these books demand readers who have active imaginations because we'll need to walk in the shoes of people who live differently than we do here and now. The reading will also require incredible amounts of brain power. We'll often need to keep maps and timelines beside us and to draw on all we know about governments and power, resistance and freedom."

As you describe the possible story lines and settings of historical fiction, you are simultaneously igniting your children's passion for books. They will learn from you that these books transport them. In every classroom where we see children on fire about books, we find a teacher who has ignited that flame with his or her visible passion.

Be sure that you do have maps on hand during this unit. You can make timelines with the students.

Remind children that earlier, they learned that journeys are better when shared. Invite them to share these new journeys not just with one partner but with a club.

"Readers, you will remember that earlier this year, I told you that my trip to Washington DC felt hollow and ho-hum until I recruited a friend to join me. You'll want traveling companions on the trips you'll take in these books. These will be *some trips*, so I'm thinking you might want to journey with not only a reading *partner* but also with a whole reading *club*. There is so much to notice and to figure out in these stories that you're going to want the combined imaginations and brainpower of a reading club. Each of you will bring something special to your club, and together, you'll see more in the books than you ever would alone. I know that as we read *Rose Blanche*, we talked about so much more than I ever would have if I had been alone.

This session launches a new social structure, book clubs, as well as a new unit of study, so your first few minilessons will need to straddle these two new endeavors. You'll see that this minilesson especially emphasizes book clubs. We considered launching clubs by showing a tiny video clip of a book club to children and strongly recommend you consider doing that. There are videos of clubs on the DVD accompanying this series. We especially suggest you show your children the footage of fourth graders discussing My Name Is Maria Isabel *because the children are extraordinarily kind and collaborative. You can ask children to join you as researchers, watching that video to study what kids need to learn to do to participate in a successful club.*

Alternatively, you could launch your discussion of book clubs by telling children about your own reading club, if you belong to one, or by inviting children to watch as you and your colleagues hold a tiny book club conversation at the front of the meeting area. One way or another, you'll want to create a drumroll to rally children's enthusiasm for this unit of study, and you can do so with great sincerity because the combination of clubs and historical fiction makes this unit into a surefire hit.

Clubs generate a tremendous amount of social energy, and you'll want to maximize and tap into this energy. You'll see that over and over in this unit, I'm recommending that you spotlight what one club has done so that others can learn from that one club. This, of course, will rally clubs to be inventive and help kids feel ownership over this social structure, this unit, and their reading lives.

"I think, readers, that some of you have been in book clubs before. And almost all of us have been in clubs of one sort or another. Maybe it's a club with our friends, or a club formed around an activity we love, like hiking or camping. And a lot of us have read *stories* about kids who are in clubs! So my question now is this: Are you willing for this class to *invent ideas* for what reading clubs can be like *for us, for the kids in this room?* There are tons of reading clubs for adults—Oprah's is the most famous—but the world hasn't invented that many ideas for how reading clubs can go for *kids*. So I'm thinking we should function as a think tank. That's like a research group where people study something and get smarter. We could grow ideas that we could share with the world for what reading clubs might be like *for kids*. What do you think?"

Not surprisingly, the response was unanimous.

Name your teaching point. Specifically, teach children that members of a club do two important things. We take care of relationships within that club, and we think about challenging things to do together.

"Readers, as we begin to invent ideas about reading clubs, I want to also teach you that it's important, in any club, to take care of relationships within that club. We do that by making sure that we're creating work where each member will feel a part of something important, and where each member will always feel supported by the group."

You can decide if you want to suggest to kids that the world needs them to invent ideas for book clubs. For me, it is always true that when I work with kids (and teachers), they help me invent ideas, and I suspect that both the teachers and kids rise to the occasion because their contributions are critical, and their good ideas are influential. All of us, as human beings, invest ourselves especially when we feel that our contributions are needed and noticed. I hope that your classroom becomes a seed bed for ideas that you do share with others, that you and your colleagues meet often to share inventions that come from one classroom or another, that kids visit each other's classrooms to see cool new things that people have invented and that you and your kids host clubs with parents, invite in kids and teachers from other schools to watch your clubs, and post videos of club conversations on your school website.

It is crucial that kids have input into the composition of these clubs, so well before this minilesson, you'll need to ask each child to write to you about the people with whom that child might want to read. Encourage them to consider reading with classmates who may be reading books that are just a bit harder or easier than the books they've been reading. Although you needn't discuss this with the children, the truth is that book clubs provide enough scaffolding that they can support a broader swath of readers working in synchrony than can partnerships.

If this teaching point seems a bit vague and broad, don't be surprised. The start of any unit needs to be encompassing. This teaching point needs to issue a generous invitation. There needs to be a sense that we are welcoming people, with great hospitality, helping them enter into and feel at home in the new unit.

TEACHING

Explain that you've already grouped children into clubs (based on their prior input), and show them that club mates are already sitting near each other.

"Recently, you wrote me a letter suggesting the names of kids with whom you'd like to read. I used those requests and also my knowledge of each of you to put you into book clubs that I think you are going to find are amazing. They'll also be a bit surprising. Try to trust me on this. I've thought really hard about ways to make up these clubs.

"Your club mates are the people with whom you read yesterday. As you can see, you are *already sitting* with your club mates."

Interview two children to learn what they do in clubs outside of school, inviting the class to brainstorm how they might do similar things within book clubs.

"Eyes on me. You needn't face your club mates just now." I waited until I had the children's attention. "If we are going to invent ideas for book clubs, we might start by thinking about the clubs we know in the world. We might ask, 'What is it about clubs that make them special?' Then we might ask, 'Which of those ideas might make sense for our book clubs?'

"To get us thinking, I thought I would ask some questions of a few classmates who have been in different kinds of clubs. Have your notebook open, because as they say things, you'll begin to have your own ideas for your club, based on your own experiences or ideas you've had from stories you've read. I'm going to do that, too. I'm going to jot some ideas in my notebook.

"Grace belongs to a gymnastics club, and Kobe to a Boy Scouts club. As you listen to me interviewing them about their clubs, think, 'Does this spark an idea for something *our* club could do?' Scrawl any ideas you get right into your reading notebook.

I signaled for Grace to join me at the front of the meeting area and asked her to tell us about her gymnastics club. "Well, we're called The Spinners," she started, "and we wear. . . ."

Technical details such as these can swamp your teaching. I worked hard to devise a plan that feels streamlined and that, I hope, will abbreviate the moments of discovering who gets whom to bypass the sighs and cheers that have a staggering capacity to hurt. I encourage you to figure out your own ways to handle this, including doing it outside the minilesson. A fiction writer once said, "The hardest thing in writing fiction is getting each character from here to there." Of course, this is also one of the hardest things about teaching! I think we need to plan the details of classroom management rather as one might plan the details of a wedding.

As time goes on in your year, you'll probably have an increasing feeling that you are turning more of your minilessons (as well as more of your reading workshop as a whole) over to the children. You'll more often interview kids, rely on transcripts of your kids' conversations, and ask a small group to perform while others watch. Always, study ways in which your minilesson does and does not seem to reach kids, and do more of whatever works. If this sort of teaching works—interviewing a child, for example— then do more of it. If you decide to interview kids fairly often in minilessons, keep in mind that you can make asides that pop out the transferable tips you hope the observing kids glean. Keep in mind also that the minilesson needs to be abbreviated so kids have giant chunks of time to read and to talk about reading, which means you'll need a signal for cutting kids short.

I intervened. Holding my thumb up as if to indicate this was now the first item on a list of ideas that could be drawn from Grace's example, I named what I hoped everyone had ascertained so far. "So your club has a name? And that's something some kids might decide to do with their clubs—give themselves a name?" Grace nodded. I pressed for some details about her process. "How did you come up with the name?"

Grace said, "The name had to deal with what we do—gymnastics. We thought of a bunch of names—like we thought of The Flippers, but that sounded like seals. We had about twenty names on a list. We wanted to come up with a name that made us sound like something we admire, or that was sort of a symbol. Actually, we got sort of stuck in a discussion that was going nowhere, and some people started to get upset. And then our coach reminded us that it was as important not to be competitive and to be good to each other as it was to pick a good name. So we just put the names on a list and did a silent vote, so nobody's feelings were hurt and we could get to practice!"

I interrupted Grace and said, "Okay, so you came up with lots of possible names (each of which fits with what you do), and then you chose one, making sure that nobody's feelings got hurt and that you didn't waste time arguing? That gives me some ideas too. Let me just jot for a second. I think I'm going to write 'names as symbols.' I like that idea. Oh, and 'come up with ways to hear everyone and not get stuck.'"

"We decided what to wear to our meets. No one could buy new stuff, so we figured out the colors we all had and decided when to wear our colors. We already knew we were meeting Sunday and Tuesday afternoons, but we decided how our meetings would go—like if we want to always start with the same warm-up routine, and if we want to write down plans and all. And food."

At this point, I said, "Wait, wait, I need to write! I love that idea of teaching each other. It reminds me of the time I was in the cooking club and someone tried to teach me how to write with frosting! I didn't really master it, but I love that idea of teaching each other new skills. Hmm . . . and I'm thinking about that idea of what to do if people get competitive. I need to think about that more. Okay, Grace, I know there are other things you do as a club, but this has already been so great! People are scrawling ideas like mad, just from what you have said.

You can prepare the children whom you will interview so they talk about things that you believe will be helpful to members of book clubs. I suspect you will want your clubs to give themselves names, to plan how they'll handle their materials (deciding whether they'll have a club folder, for example) and to think about whether they want to begin or end their meetings with certain rituals. Of course, the names and materials and rituals will be different if the club is a chess club or a rugby club rather than a reading club. In the end, you're picturing that your readers might name themselves something like The Dust Bowl and might invent rituals such as starting each meeting with members laying out their best ideas (in the form of their best Post-its) on the table and the club deciding to select one idea to talk at length about.

Notice how I rearticulate what the student has just said, wording the concept of trying on different club names for size before selecting the best one in a fashion that I hope makes this transferable to book clubs. I am popping out the concept I want the listeners to take from this interview.

Ideas for clubs
meet often
help eachother
Practice stuff
teach new skills
get a logo/insignia

"Let's hear from Kobe." I signaled for Kobe to take Grace's place and began by asking him, "Are there big ways in which Boy Scout clubs are different than Grace's gymnastics club?"

Kobe started by saying, "In my troop, we have an oath that we have to memorize: 'On my honor I will do my best to do my duty to. . . .' And we have an insignia that means stuff."

"The insignia. Is that like a logo?"

"Yeah, and it has an eagle on it for democracy and stuff like that. And we can earn merit badges, too. And we plan things to do, like service projects and hikes."

"So you plan things to do—things that go with the main themes of your club, is that it?" I asked.

Ask each child to reflect on clubs he or she has been in and to mine memories of those clubs to jot yet more ideas for how their new club should go.

By this time, I was ready to turn this over to the class. "I've seen you guys writing like crazy, ideas that come from what Grace and Kobe have said. Right now, before your club meets to talk, think about clubs *you've* been in—and especially think about *reading* clubs you've been in, if you've been in them before—and jot more ideas for how this year's club can be the best in the world. Do that now."

ACTIVE INVOLVEMENT

Channel children to meet with club mates to talk together about ideas they've been gleaning (and writing) for how their club might go, constructing a constitution.

"I can tell that you have a lot of ideas you want to share with your fellow club members. Why don't you turn to your club and tell each other some of the important ideas you gleaned from hearing what Grace and Kobe have been doing in their clubs, and from mining your own memories of past clubs you've been in."

After children talked for longer than the usual interval, I said, "Will you and your club mates record ideas you have for how to make your book club work? When the United

You can say, "I know people are scrawling ideas like mad" even if that is a bit of an exaggeration. Remember Harste's quotation: "I see our job as creating, in classrooms, the kind of world we believe in and then inviting children to role-play their way into being the readers and writers we want them to be." You can act as if your kids are totally enthralled and engaged as a way to scaffold your children into being just this. And if your goal is to nudge kids to take notes as they listen to these interviews, saying, "I see many of you scrawling like mad, recording ideas that Grace and Kobe have given you for your club," will probably work better than saying, "Children. Remember you were told to write notes. I have only seen two of you do that. The rest of you need to get started right now." You are hoping to engage them in this new adventure of book clubs, not to force them to complete an assignment.

Notice that I don't reiterate the things that are not pertinent to book clubs, and I rephrase what the child says so that I make his ideas more transferable to book clubs. I take, "We plan service projects and hikes," and restate this as, "You plan things to do that go with the main themes of your club." Notice, too, all the ways I move this along so that we stay on schedule.

Today, more than usual, your job is to be the head cheerleader among children, rallying their enthusiasm and excitement about book clubs. The teachers who piloted these sessions found that this early "gearing up" work helped children stay deeply invested in their clubs throughout the rest of the unit. The social structure of clubs has the capacity to light your room on fire, and you want to do everything possible to make that happen. One way I rally kids' energy is to act as if they already have it—hence the line, "I've seen you guys writing like crazy." That may well be an overstatement!

You may want to reveal a record of some of the talk possibilities for your kids.

States of America was formed, people like Thomas Jefferson, Ben Franklin, and John Adams gathered in a little room in Philadelphia to talk over the plan for a new nation, and they wrote our Constitution. You are talking over plans not for a new nation, but for a new club, and you, like those guys, will end up writing a sort of constitution. You'll need a sheet of notebook paper or two to record plans for things you will do together, but don't actually *do* those things now. For now, make a to-do list. You could write, 'We should find a name' but wait 'til later today to actually find that name. Later you'll have time to do the things on your list." I distributed a guide sheet that I hoped would support the conversation:

Creating a Constitution for Our Club

- What will we call ourselves?

- What will our rituals be—our ways of working?

- Will we decide how many pages to read before the next meeting? At the start of the book? At the end of each meeting? Or do we want to plan a calendar of reading assignments in advance to save time and help people organize their lives?

- How can our writing about reading help us bring our ideas together? Will club members write in whatever form works for us (Post-its, letters, entries, charts), or will we decide on a form for the club?

- Will we always decide on a sub-topic to address (e.g., how the character is changing) or only sometimes?

As children talked and worked, I voiced over a few pointers. "Remember that your club will be a *reading* club, so if you decide to give your club a name, for example, you'll want the name to relate to reading. And if you come up with rituals, they can't take time away from reading work."

After children talked for a bit, I said, "All eyes on me" and waited for their attention before continuing.

Notice how I slip some teaching about history into this discussion of children's book club constitutions and then draw a connection between the likes of Thomas Jefferson and the children. I want children to understand that people's decisions have big effects. I want them to treat their book clubs with reverence, believing that these little groups can create big, powerful thinking.

- Name:

- What should we discuss? : We should discuss the changes that is happening in the book.

- What How will we decide what to talk about? : We will decide by looking through our notes and pulling out the ones that tie together into a main idea.

- What should we write about/should we write the same thing? : yes we should write about the characters personalities and feelings.

- How far should we read each night? It depends. if we are at a really challenging part in the book I would make the goal a lot shorter because I might want to go back and reread.

- How many times we should discuss a week?

- How to make the talk more detailed and interesting?

You may find it difficult to get hold of readers' attention at this point. Remember that their chattiness is probably the result of their heightened excitement. They are taking the reins of their reading lives in a whole new way. You won't want their chattiness to interfere with the minilesson, but go easy. Enthusiasm will be more helpful than dutifulness.

Ask children to consider how being part of a club will make them read differently, and then share out one club's thinking.

"Readers, although you will be part of clubs, you'll still spend most of the reading workshop reading your own independent books. One thing you will definitely want to think about is this: How will you read differently because you are part of your club? How will each of you collect ideas that you can discuss later? Talk with your club mates and see if you can invent a plan for how you'll read *differently* because you'll be in a club together. Will you plan out the questions you'll carry with you as you read? Do a particular form of jotting? Give each other assignments for what everyone's going to think and write about—or what?"

As children talked with each other, I listened. After a bit, I convened the group. "Class, listen to the smart ideas that Sarah and her club were just talking about."

Sarah said, "We were talking about how we could help each other, like we could figure out what people are good at, like how we talked about people's reading talents when we were finishing *The Tiger Rising*. Well, if someone is good at reading a lot, then she could help others do that, and if someone is good at making connections, then she could help others do that. Maybe after every talk she could say, 'This connects to our read-aloud book because . . . ,' and she could be The Connector.'"

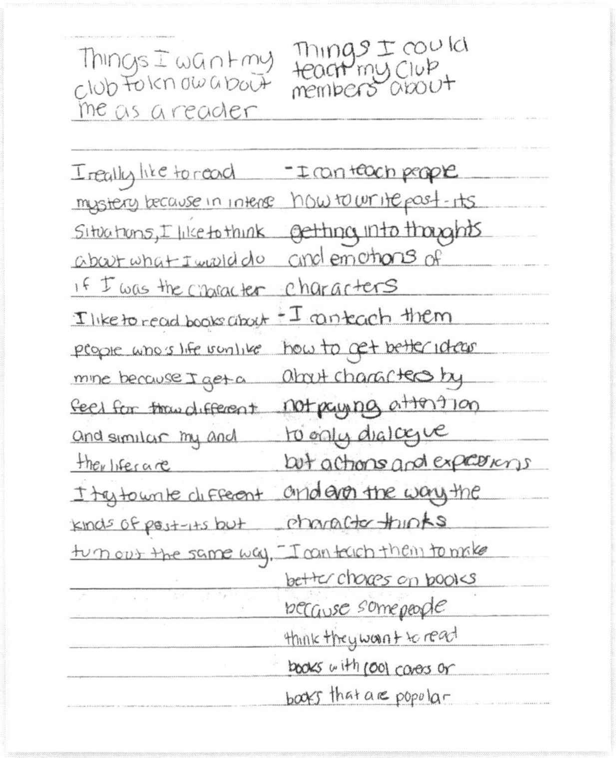

"That's a smart idea, isn't it? The members of Sarah's club are going to spend some time writing and then talking about the talents each one has that he or she could bring to the club. *[Fig. II-1]* Your club may want to borrow that idea. And also, the rest of you will have your own cool ideas for how your club will go—and we'll want to hear those as well."

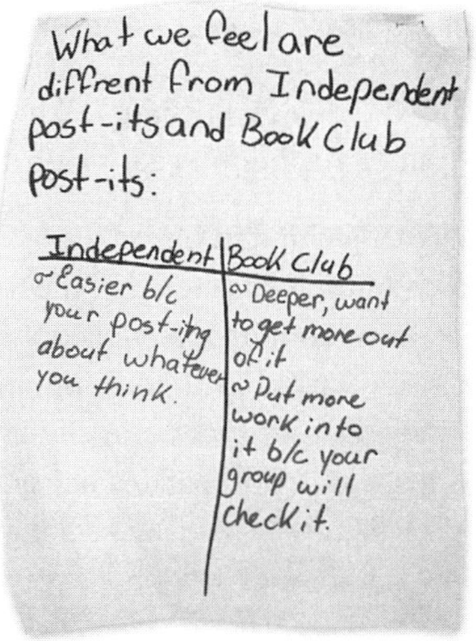

Figure II-1

LINK

Send children off to spend today's workshop talking about the items on their to-do list. Explain that you'll circulate, helping each club select an era and related books.

"So, readers, today marks the start of your clubs. You'll be reading multiple copies of books, with everyone in the club reading the same book and progressing in sync through that book, and you'll be talking about those books with members of your club. This means that your club will need to make some decisions about the books you want to read and about the time period in history in which you want to immerse yourselves. I know many of you are still reading and talking about the picture book you started yesterday. You'll finish reading and talking about it today, and I'll come around to each club to show you some of the options you have for time periods and books you decide to read.

"But for now, I suggest that instead of getting started on *reading*, you take time to get started on *being part of a club*. You've given yourselves a list of work to do. Most of you want to name your club, to make some sort of a binder to hold your work, to think about the sort of writing you plan to do as you read, to decide where you want your meeting space to be. So how about, for now, you spread out just a bit while basically staying in this general vicinity and, instead of reading, you talk? If you decide upon another place to meet regularly, you can move to that place. I'll be coming around and telling you about some of the amazing books you might choose to read."

You will have noticed by now the degree of choice we are giving children. They are responsible for organizing their club's materials, meeting place, book selections, and even the club's name! This group work simultaneously fosters a lot of accountability. Giving children these liberties allows them to author lives in which reading matters, a thread that has been woven throughout these units.

Though it's true your children will have many choices to make, their book picks will be limited by the selection you have in your classroom. You may find that you have only two choices of eras in which you have books that match a particular club's reading level abilities. Therefore, be prepared to talk up the time periods around which your books cluster. This shouldn't be a hard sell since so many of the books children will read during this unit will be full of fun facts and journeys—whether they are set during a war or during Westward Expansion or during any other historical episode.

CONFERRING AND SMALL-GROUP WORK

Rally Youngsters to Invest in Books Clubs—Deeply

The conferring sections in this book will often address your work with book clubs, because they will be the newest structure in your reading workshop, and therefore they'll be the structure that occupies most of your thinking. You'll probably ask children to sit near club mates as they read so that, if you so choose, you can ask members of a club to talk together during silent reading time, while you are able to observe and coach them, and then to read silently during the time when others will be in clubs. This flexibility means that at least for now, at the start of club work, a great percentage of your conferring will be devoted to getting your clubs well launched.

The Importance of Rallying Clubs to Tackle Self-Selected Goals

Researchers have actually found that when teachers lead small-group work, more often than not, what the teacher does with one small group is what the teacher does with another small group (Allington 2006). The irony is that we all believe small

---

MID-WORKSHOP TEACHING POINT

Club Members Discuss Hopes and Potential Problems

"As I told you earlier, when people join together to form organizations—whether these are teams, nations, or clubs—people often write a constitution. We think, 'How can we work together in ways that will meet everyone's hopes?' and 'How can we plan ways to deal with the predictable problems?' We put some of our vows, our plans, onto the paper.

"When people write constitutions, part of what we do is anticipate common questions and predictable problems, talking through our thoughts about both. I've watched other kids, other years, in clubs, and it seems to me there are some predictable problems, and it profits us to discuss them. Take a look at this chart to help you think through possible problems that may come up during club conversations—and ways to address them. You may want to discuss other potential problems and potential solutions, based on your own experiences. Be sure that your constitution includes your plan for how you'll deal with the problems you anticipate."

Anticipate and Invent Responses to Predictable Problems in Book Clubs

- If someone does not do his or her reading, how can the rest of us help that reader keep up?

- If we want to read beyond the page number set by the club, yet don't want to get ahead of our club-mates, what can we do with our extra reading time? Should we shift to other historical fiction books or should we read nonfiction related to the same time period?

- When we can't all agree, how will we settle our differences so that we don't waste club time?

- How will we bring out the quiet voices while still leaning on the ideas of those who are active contributors?

continued on next page

---

groups are important because they allow us to be responsive to individual differences, yet often, one small group marches along in sync with the next. More than this, usually all these small groups involve small groups all trying to accomplish what is essentially a whole-class assignment.

One of the constants in American education has been that the teacher doles out a task, and everyone does that task at the same time. The teacher waits until everyone is done, and then doles out the next task. There are obvious problems to this. To grasp the problems you need only imagine if teachers in your school were all asked to teach in lockstep, with someone doling out precisely what each teacher was to do, with the expectation that each teacher was to do the same thing at the same time and in the same way, and then the whole school waited until everyone accomplished that one task before the next task was doled out. It is unlikely that such a regimen would tap into anyone's energy for learning, and certainly there would be little possibility that individuals could respond thoughtfully to the specifics they encountered. Readers, like teachers, do not all need or want to do the same thing at the same time, in sync with each other, and expecting students to do this is not apt to tap into their talent, enthusiasm, or energy. But, of course, there are advantages. First among these is that such a structure is easy to manage, and it is easy to keep track of what students are doing.

You have a choice. You can lead reading clubs in such a way that although members of one of your clubs might start by reading *Sarah, Plain and Tall* while members of another might be reading *Bud, Not Buddy*, readers in both those clubs and in every other club in your classroom are engaged in the same work on the same day, applied to different books. You can do a bit of work with the read-aloud, and each day say, "Today, I want each of you do this same work with your book."

I don't recommend a steady regimen of this, though. You'll be bored. Your kids will be bored. Instead, in this unit, go to great lengths to help readers know that their club is just that—their club. They can decide with each other (and yes, with you) upon goals they'll tackle and ways they'll work, just as you do with your colleagues. And one club will be distinct from another because day in and day

MID-WORKSHOP TEACHING POINT

continued from previous page

Children talked within their clubs, fast and furiously, with lots of passion. Five minutes into the conversation, I inserted a quick comment. "Club members," I said, waiting until I had their attention. "Be conscious of whether you all are caring for each other right now, in this conversation. If this relationship is going to work, it needs to be built on a foundation of care. Use the challenge of writing a club constitution as a way to figure out how to talk so you really listen, so all voices are heard, so you grow ideas together that are better than what any of you could do on your own. Get back to your conversations."

Especially in these early days of setting up club rules and regulations, children will benefit from reminders to treat each other with equity and care. Even though you've given children a great deal of autonomy and trust, the truth is they are still nine, ten, or eleven years old.

At another point, I voiced over the hubbub, saying, "Be sure you capture your club's plans on paper. If you need paper or markers or folders, I've added those items to the writing center." [Fig 11-2]

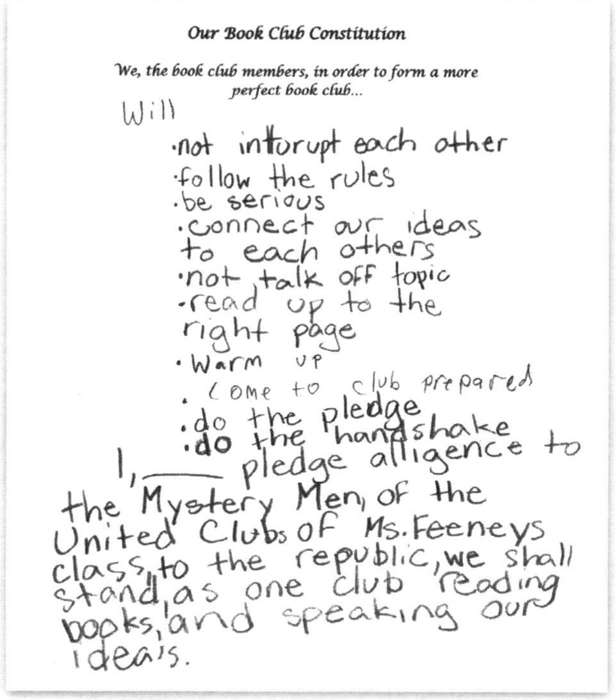

Our Book Club Constitution

We, the book club members, in order to form a more perfect book club...

Will

- not inturupt each other
- follow the rules
- be serious
- connect our ideas to each others
- not talk off topic
- read up to the right page
- warm up
- come to club prepared
- do the pledge
- do the handshake
- do pledge alligence to

I,_____ the Mystery Men, of the United Clubs of Ms. Feeneys class, to the republic, we shall stand, as one club reading books, and speaking our ideas.

Figure II-2

out, readers will make decisions about the work they want to do together.

Because each club will be distinct, the work each club engages in will have the potential to invigorate the culture of the classroom. If a club or two generates some energy around one kind of reading work—say, reading aloud with fluency—that energy will be contagious, and those children will be in positions to teach others the remarkable things they've done.

You may be uneasy about this entire plan. But think for a moment about this question: What is the worst thing that could happen? After all, your kids will still be reading quietly for thirty to forty minutes a day. Instead of meeting with a partner for five minutes, they'll meet with a club for what, ten minutes? Fifteen? During that time they'll do some reading aloud, they'll talk about their observations, they'll read aloud the writing about reading they've done, and so on. If you give them some leeway to make decisions about how to talk together and about how to angle their reading work, what's the worst thing that could happen?

Meanwhile, consider the best that could happen. The best is that book clubs can allow you to scaffold children to work with enormous resolve and a sense of personal agency to develop reading skills that you and they, together, decide are important. Ideally, clubs will tap the power of the social fabric of your classroom in the service of these reading goals. Meanwhile, the classroom community can become enriched by the grand buzzing diversity of work that is occurring and by the fact that different children will become skilled at different things, allowing children to emerge as stars, famous for their contributions on all sorts of different fronts. And all the while, at home and in school, children will be immersed in a genre that illuminates the intersection of nonfiction and fiction, of social studies and English, and that helps them progress along in trajectories of skill development.

Responding to Predictable Problems

Of course, all of that drum roll sounds Pollyanna-like, and the truth is that there are predictable problems you are sure to encounter with clubs, and pretending otherwise is not going to make those problems go away. Now, early on in this unit, you'll need to "put on roller skates" so that you can move quickly among clubs, just as earlier in the year you moved quickly among individual readers.

Foremost on your list should be an awareness that often when children join book clubs, talking about books becomes the main event in the reading classroom, and reading itself can get lost. You'll definitely want to be sure that children continue to maintain their reading logs, taking these between home and school, and that they record not only their progress through the club's shared book but also the reading they do on the side. Are children reading something like three-quarters of a page a minute for at least an hour a day, in and out of school? If not, this should make you uneasy. Then, too, by this time in the year, you should expect that many of your children will sometimes read long past the minimum number of pages or minutes. If a child never gets caught up in a story, this should make you uneasy.

If you see that volume and pace seem to be problems, don't waste a minute before researching what the underlying issue may be. Sometimes writing about reading swamps reading itself, in which case you may want to suggest that kids limit themselves to writing only quick jotted notes, save for perhaps one day a week when they write long and strong, or you may want to suggest that they read for long chunks and then write as a reflective move after doing that reading. Note whether readers who are

not getting through a lot of books are reading appropriate books. How is their fluency? [Fig. II-3]

Then, too, sometimes the invitation to participate in book clubs can seem to be an invitation to mayhem. Engaged conversation is one thing—mayhem, another. You may need to actively and assertively teach your students how to collaborate productively. Start today. You will have channeled readers to devote most of the day to long conversations about each other's hopes and dreams for their club. Just because kids won't be holding books in hand doesn't mean they won't profit from your coaching them toward the behaviors that are essential to a productive book club.

For example, there is no reason to wait before helping children make sure that they talk together in ways that can be heard. It helps for them to sit close to each other, around just a single desk rather than around a cluster of four desks, or to clump together in a huddle on the floor. If children must sit around four desks, you may need to encourage some of them to actually kneel, bottoms up, leaning over the table so that people can talk together. Of course, the seating arrangement alone won't allow people to hear each other. It will also be necessary to coach children to stop speaking into their collars in ways that make it very hard for others

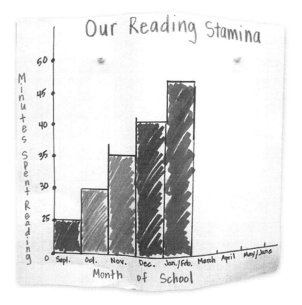

Figure II-3
This class chart captures one classroom's increasing stamina for reading.

to hear. You can be the one to say, "I'm not sure others were able to hear," but it will be more helpful if you teach children to say something similar to each other. If someone's words are being swallowed, whisper, "Can you hear?" to another club member. If the child shakes her head no, then say, "So what are you going to do to address this?" and prompt the youngster to take action. If the classroom is too loud for children to hear each other, then you could prompt a child from one club to go to another club and say, "We're having a hard time hearing each other, could you all talk more quietly?" In these ways, then, you can resist being the problem solver.

Of course, sometimes clubs will have a hard time hearing each other because the classroom is a flurry of unrest, and that will be your problem as well as your children's to solve. For starters, you may want to rethink the locations of your clubs. Might it be possible for one club to meet in the hallway or in the far corner of the classroom, behind your desk? Then, too, you might consider organizing your class so that instead of asking all children to read silently for two thirds of the workshop and for all of them to talk together for the last third of class time, some clubs meet for the first portion of the workshop and others for the last. Of course, the easiest solution is to help your children refrain from raising voices.

When Club Meetings Are Overrun with Arguments Over What the Club Will Do

Clubs require children to work collaboratively, which means they need to learn how to compromise, to share power, and to negotiate. In some classrooms, children have not had many opportunities to work in these ways, and sometimes the work involved in learning to do this threatens to derail the reading workshop for a bit. Although it might be tempting to give up on a particular class of children learning to collaborate, saying, "I still need them to learn to read, even if they are beastly to each other," it is a sad day if we give up on young people learning to get along.

The books themselves can offer children help in the work of collaborating with each other. Robert Coles talks about the power that comes from reading literature among the life-and-death, lives-on-the-line culture of a hospital. Perhaps it is almost as powerful for children to read stories about bullying and inner wounds, fears that suffocate, friends that refuse to betray each other, and to do this reading within the culture of American schools, a culture that for kids often feels as if it puts lives on the line.

Although eventually, you'll be able to talk to club members about the fact that the characters in their books offer them models for ways of working with other people, models that could perhaps inform their relationships within the club itself, for now the new books probably haven't had time to gather a head of steam enough that you can harness that power when helping kids work together in their clubs.

The answer, however, can't be for you to assume the role of peacemaker and negotiator or, more worrisome still, for you to decide that the club simply can't make decisions collaboratively and needs therefore to be controlled by you. Instead, coach the club members to find ways to solve their own problems—and do so now, when their problems are not yet about reading itself but are instead about the nature of their club. If club members can't negotiate on how to name the club, on what the logo will be, or what historical era the club will read about, and so forth, these clubs will in a few days have equal trouble deciding what to talk about and how many pages to read. Procedural talk can consume most of their club meetings if you don't intercede. You'll need to be clear that coming to a decision needs to involve minutes, not days of time. I recently said to members of two different clubs, "Here is the thing. In life, you all need to learn to work together with small groups of your peers. That is as important a goal as learning to read well, to write well. So I do not plan to solve your problems for you. You are entirely too grown up for me to need to step in. But on the other hand, you absolutely *may not* waste precious reading time haggling. When a club needs to solve something, I expect it to get done within two or three minutes. If necessary, draw straws to make a decision. A club may not waste club time arguing!"

When One or Two Kids Dominate the Conversations

You can be sure that even on this first day of your club meetings, you will worry that one or two children will be dominating some of the club conversations. I have a few bits of advice about this. First, I would refrain from repeatedly admonishing the more dominant children to say less. Your talkative children are often readers whose minds are brimful of ideas about books, and you will want those children to function as mentors and spark plugs within the group. If you pull a chair alongside a small-group conversation, and the one most assertive child is talking away with enormous detail about his or her ideas, you do not want the other children in the group to respond by rolling their eyes and thinking, "There he goes again, talking on and on." Instead, you want the other children to listen to the content of this child's comments and to jump into the talk saying, "To add on to what you said. . . ."

This doesn't mean you won't, in fact, help the dominant child say less (more on this in a minute), but if you say, "Fallon, let someone else have a turn talking," and then, a few minutes later, you say, "Fallon, could you give someone else a chance?" you will have taught all the other children to be irritated that Fallon is dominating their "air space"—and really, you want those other children to listen to her ideas and get aboard the conversation. There will be no chance that Fallon can provide an intellectual lift to the group if you've continually harped on her for dominating too much; she will no longer be able to function as the model for what it means to be an active participant. Her ideas will no longer become everyone's ideas.

So if you want to tone down the amount of talking that a dominant club member does, take that child aside and say something like, "You have the ability to talk well in a club. It is much harder to be the person who talks third or fourth in a conversation, building on some remark that a classmate just threw out into the air and going with *that person's* remark (rather than putting your own remark out at the start of a conversation). Could you try to get others to talk first about the book, and help them say more, even. And then, after others have ideas on the table, could you use your talk skills to take one of those ideas that someone else has put out and build on it?" Alternatively, you could be more direct and say to this child (but not to his or her club mates), "You are dominating a bit too much. Let's agree upon a secret signal so that if I feel like you are talking too much and need you to step down, I can give you that signal."

"Of course, you'll want to coach children not only to talk collaboratively, but also to talk with depth. Over time, you'll remind children of ways to talk with depth and to chart your suggestions."

You might suggest a particular club (or the class as a whole) take on the project of bringing out the quieter voices. Sometimes if one watches, a quieter speaker can become agitated, making some motions such as

> Playing Your Part In Deep Club Talk
>
> • Do your work to prepare for the conversation. Read up to the goal. Jot down your ideas.
>
> • Make eye contact with each other during your talk. Materials should be close at hand, but you shouldn't read or write with others are speaking.
>
> • Take turns, don't raise hands.
>
> • Take risks! Speak up and share your ideas!
>
> • Help your fellow readers build up their ideas. Ask them questions.

climbing up on his or her knees, or starting to say something; an attuned club mate can be very helpful if he or she notices these signs and says, "Did you want to add on to that?" in a way that makes space for the quieter voice to join the conversation. Similarly, once that child has said something, it is helpful if the next speaker doesn't jump in too fast on the heels of the quieter child, cutting that child short. Often after one quiet child speaks, if there is a little pool of silence, a second quiet child will speak into that silence, because for some reason it is easier to contribute when proceeding in the wake of a quiet child's comment.

It is probably too early, today, to teach club members that it can help a lot if, from time to time, someone takes it upon himself or herself to summarize where the group's conversation has gone, saying, "So far, we have talked about. . . ." Keep this tip in mind, teachers, because it is a helpful way to collect and restart a conversation that seems to be lagging or to have gotten off track.

The most important thing that happens in a club is that people listen. Clubs work when people lean in to really hear, listen hard, ask follow-up questions, and respond to what each other has to say. So rather than focusing on the goal of one person not talking, I'd suggest you focus on the goal of children really listening to each other.

TEACHING SHARE

Book Clubs Invent Ways to Share Their Books

Invite several children to speak to the class about how their clubs will function, stopping and giving the class time to jot ideas stimulated by what they've heard.

When it came time to bring the reading workshop to a close, I convened children in the meeting area so that I would have their undivided attention. Once they'd all settled down, I said, "Earlier I suggested that perhaps you could invent ideas for book clubs that would be helpful to kids the world over. I never dreamt that you might come up with those ideas on *the very first day!* I'm going to ask a couple of you to tell the rest of us your ideas for your club. If you hear something from another club that provokes an idea for your own club, scrawl that idea in your reading notebook and later you can talk about it."

As Fallon took her place at the front of the meeting area, I added, "Let me mention that a huge goal in this unit will be for all of us to become the kind of people who listen to others and grow ideas in response to what we hear. Strong readers let not only *texts* but also *other people's words* get through to us. We take in the words and ideas of others, and we think in response."

COACHING TIPS

Learn to talk in ways that command attention. Your message today is important.

The historical readers constitution

• We promise that we will all read to our goals and that everyone is comfortable with our reading point.

• If we are absent to a talk than we promise to e-mail or call a club member to talk about our reading.

• We will respect eachothers Ideas even if we disagree.

• We promise to jot and do our best thinking about our reading so we come prepared for the next talk.

• We promise to give everyone our best attention by doing eye contact, nodding, and looking interested!

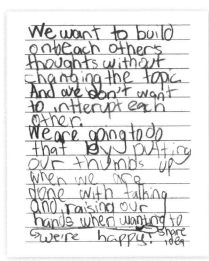

We want to build on each other's thoughts without changing the topic. And we don't want to interrupt each other. We are going to do that by putting our thumbs up when we are done with talking and raising our hands when wanting to share idea & we're happy!

Fallon took a big breath and began. "Our club is called The Freedom Fighters, and we have a motto: 'Where stories come alive!' We decided that when any one of us has read up to that night's assignment, we'll read another historic fiction on our own. We're starting by reading *Freedom Summer*, and then *The Gold Cadillac* and *Roll of Thunder, Hear My Cry*." Fallon turned to sit down.

I was about to commend this club on all their terrific ideas when Fallon added, "Oh, oh, we each have a different color of Post-it, and when we talk, we're going to put them all together, but because of the different colors, we'll know who wrote which one."

I jumped in. "Holy moly. What ideas! Let me give the rest of us a minute to scrawl all the millions of ideas that are no doubt coming to your mind for your reading club as you listen," and I started scrawling like mad myself.

If you are wondering how this club came up with so many great ideas, you need to remember that the teacher can prepare a club to demonstrate whatever it is you want the club to demonstrate.

You asked children to take notes of what others say. When children talk, be sure you demonstrate this yourself. Listen intently with pen poised, letting the comments children say spark ideas in you, and then record these ideas. If you do not see others doing this as well, be prepared to call children on this. In all ways, make sure your words are not disregarded. If no one is taking notes when you asked them to do so, you really have no choice but to take this up as a cause (even if it is to decide as a class that your instructions to take notes actually don't make sense and should be abandoned). Otherwise, you inadvertently contribute to the notion that kids are made of Teflon—that it is okay if nothing anyone says gets through to them. Keep in mind, too, that accountable talk can characterize the entire school day, not just book discussions.

After the children scrawled for a moment, I voiced over their continued work. "As you jot your thoughts, I want to add that it's a really cool idea to read yet another picture book, this one pertaining to the era your club will study, because it'll give you a quick sense of the kind of books we'll be reading—of historical fiction—and also because after just a day, you'll already be able to talk across books. So some of you may decide to do that."

Remember that if you'd like an idea to become the talk of your town, you can confer with someone, finding a way to help that individual or that person generate the idea. Then later you can ask that person or that club to share ideas with the class, knowing the idea you nurtured will this way become disseminated. This allows you to steer a bit from behind. If no one voices the idea you'd like, you could always say, "The classes that came before you have left a legacy of their smart thinking in this room. Let me share some of the ideas kids came up with last year—ideas that made last year's book clubs work well." You could also say, "If some of these ideas could help your club, go ahead and write them down. Remember that you will also leave a legacy for future students."

I then motioned for a spokesperson from a second club to come to the front of the meeting area. Kwami took a big breath and then, all in a rush of words, said, "Our club is The Dust Bowl, since we're gonna read lots of books that take place in the Depression, but we

In the interest of time, you'll probably ask just one person from no more than two clubs to share. Other club members will want to contribute, too. Be prepared to signal no.

don't want to call ourselves Depressed Readers! We want to make sure we compliment everyone's Post-its before we start talking so we're going to lay them out and then go around and read them and then give everyone a compliment."

Ask clubs to make plans for the night's reading work.

At this point, I regained the reins. "Talk with your club-mates now about two things. First, talk about new ideas you now have for your club, and second, talk about your reading assignment for tonight. You might try The Freedom Fighters' idea and read a picture book that goes with your era, if there is one, or you could do some nonfiction related to your era if you'd like. If it is just as easy, I'd be pleased if you waited to start your first big chapter book tomorrow, because our minilesson will help you get started. Either way, be sure you clarify the reading work you'll do tonight. Whatever you decide, make sure you continue to fill in your reading logs. New units don't change our continuing routines!"

Notice that I engineered the content that was shared to channel children toward reading a picture book tonight. The real reason for that is that the upcoming minilesson is meant to help children as they embark on reading a historical fiction novel, so I wanted to steer them away from starting their chapter books at home tonight. This is not, of course, crucial.

IN THIS SESSION,
you will teach your students
that readers keep track of
story elements as we read,
continually building our
understanding of what's
going on.

Synthesizing Story Elements

ven if you do not go so far as to launch adult book clubs to accompany this unit, try this. Pick up one of the historical fiction books that your kids will be reading, and read the first three pages of it. Then pause and name what it was you were doing as you read. You will have done tons of intellectual work, and you won't be able to name everything you've done, so try to capture the main work that you found your mind doing as you proceeded through those first pages. Now take a different historical fiction book and repeat the process, noticing whether the work that you are doing in the second text is similar to that which you did in the first. Note, too, ways in which your reading process is different now that you are reading historical fiction in contrast to, say, realistic fiction.

When my colleagues and I were ready to launch this unit, we did exactly as I've just described. We sat in the company of each other—there were about ten of us—and we read. Then we paused to name the mind work that we'd been doing. We tried to reach for accurate, precise words and to resist relying on the code words for reading comprehension that sometimes obscure more than they reveal. Instead of saying, "I was envisioning the setting" or "I was inferring," we tried to open up vague terms by naming precisely what we were doing.

GETTING READY

- Select a text to read aloud throughout this unit. I've chosen *Number the Stars*. If you worry that the book is too heavy or complex for a third-grade class, know that many third-grade classes did work with this book and found it to be magical. We include other suggested read-alouds on the *Resources for Teaching Reading* CD-ROM.

- Rest a large piece of construction paper on the tray of your easel during the minilesson to act as your 'mental bulletin board.' You may want to scrawl a few bits of information on papers that you will tack onto it to create a visual accompaniment to the minilesson.

- Place maps and globes near children's reading places so they may note the locations of their stories.

- Finish *Rose Blanche* before this session and have the book next to you for the minilesson teaching point. You can, of course, teach a different point.

- Prepare a chart titled "Making Our Way Through Historical Fiction" to unveil during the mid-workshop teaching point.

- Pace your read-aloud so you will have finished the first chapter of *Number the Stars* by the following session. You won't read all of Chapter 1 within this minilesson. In general, you'll see that the minilessons suggest you progress extremely slowly through *Number the Stars*, which is less than ideal; you may want to read picture books aloud simultaneously, outside the reading workshop.

We expected that because historical fiction sweeps readers up and sets us down in another time and place, we would especially find ourselves envisioning, building the world of the story. We anticipated that we'd read with our skin inside out, extra alert to any sense of atmosphere, to any sensory words, ready to use those words to generate a sensory-rich world, full of sights and sounds and tastes and tones. This is the sort of reading work we'd helped readers to do while they were reading picture books. But when we

> *How important it is for us to teach readers that reading involves not only being swept up by a story but also accumulating information!*

were reading the first two chapters of our historical fiction books, most of us felt that in these complex texts, there was too much new information coming at us during those early pages for us to really generate mental movies just yet. Instead, the reading work we found ourselves doing, where we gathered up all the story essentials, felt like tacking elements up onto a bulletin board. We would read and meet one character—say, in *Number the Stars*, Annemarie. We'd tack that name up on a mental bulletin board and read on, finding a second name—Ellen. Soon we'd tacked a few details under each name: Annemarie is blonde, leggy, an athlete. Ellen: short, brown-haired, a scholar. We'd tack up the places, too: Copenhagen. And mentally, alongside that, we'd jot some details: a city, Denmark. Then a new charac-

ter: the little sister. Still unnamed, she goes on the mental board, with questions beside her. Whose sister is she? What's her name? What's she like? And on we'd read.

Of course, we no sooner tacked elements onto the bulletin board than they began to morph. The little sister is actually *Annemarie's* younger sibling. Her name is Kristi. She and Annemarie have a bigger sister, too, who is not present and around whom there is some mystery. Now a question gets added to the board: Why is the big sister introduced and then not mentioned? Where is the big sister? The main characters, too, began to morph: Ellen is not only short, brown-haired, and a scholar, but she also lives in an apartment above Annemarie. She is proud of being a good student.

Other things were happening as we read. For example, I found that as I passed my eyes over content-specific words such as *Copenhagen* or *Nazi occupation* or *the Resistance*, it was as if I'd pressed a link on my computer screen. Everything I knew related to those key words surfaced for me, forming an ecosystem of background information behind my tacked-together mental construction. I was aware that the kids would probably draw on less background information, but figured the process of drawing on what one knows would always be a part of reading anything and especially of reading historical fiction.

We found ourselves learning more as we read. Thinking about this afterward, my colleagues and I realized that strong readers accumulate information about the science, geography, and history during reading—and others do not. A strong reader who reads *American Girl* books, for example, not only finds out how Felicity saves the day or how Kit makes a friend, but she also finds out how to make butter, how to calm bees to get honey, and how to get blood from a pricked finger. When reading harder books, the reader often has to learn some new information at the start of the book to make sense of what is happening right after that. We realized, too, that it takes deliberate effort on the part of a reader to "read to learn" rather than just sweeping through plots. This way of reading, where a reader rapidly

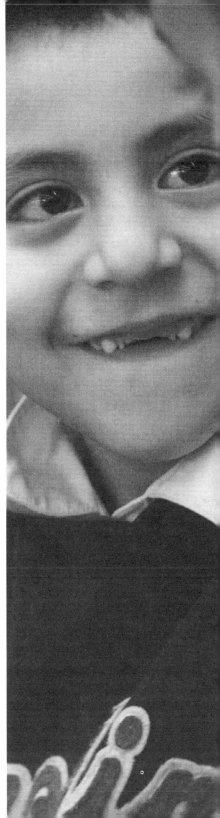

accumulates and uses new information, will be especially essential in historical fiction. Our reflections on our own reading led us to think that just as Jack in the *Magic Treehouse* books keeps a notebook where he records what he learns on his adventures, we would probably want to show children how to take notes about what they are learning in the stories they devour.

Of course, while learning about the places in a historical fiction book, we also learn about the characters. Often the information that a reader notices first is that which separates one character from another, giving them roles to play. As we read on, though, with just a bit of deliberate digging, it is not hard to also collect information on the pressures that the main character experiences, the issues that surround that person. Because history puts challenges in the protagonist's path, we found that aspects of the plot are almost implicit in the historical setting.

As my colleagues and I talked about challenges we faced when reading complex texts and studied the texts that our students were reading, we were reminded that when readers read novels that are in or beyond the R/S/T band of difficulty, readers need to continually and quickly accumulate information about the characters, the setting, and the story's main issues and problems. Details matter in these books, and readers need to notice the details right away in order to use them to read between the lines. Also, the details will often shift with some rapidity. In these more complex novels, the information that a reader collects isn't always explicit, and it will tend to be interspersed throughout the story rather than coming all in one passage. When I was two-thirds of the way through *Number the Stars* (a level U book), I was still continuing to learn new information about the recent death of Lise, Annemarie's big sister, and about the activities of Peter, her sister's fiancé. How important, then, it is for us to teach readers that reading involves not only being swept up by a story but also accumulating information!

Here is my bigger point. As books become more complex, the task of getting one's arms around the story line is, in and of itself, challenging. Although the children will think of this as a unit on reading historical fiction, the real aim is to help them read more complex texts. Although the unit will progress toward supporting interpretive reading, this first bend of the unit teaches essentials of comprehension, and it does so by revisiting and extending skills that readers were taught in the first two units. For example, constructing theories about a character's traits is easier when the character is Harry in the book *Horrible Harry* than when the character is Sistine, from *The Tiger Rising*, who resolutely refuses to be pegged, or Percy Jackson, from *The Lightning Thief*, who is confused himself. It is easier to develop theories about a character if the author does that work for the reader, early in the book, and if the character generally acts in ways that are consistent with those early descriptors. It is more challenging to develop theories about characters if readers see a character through the eyes of different people, each of whom sees (and reveals) a different side of that character, if information about the character keeps emerging, or if the character is inconsistent, saying one thing and doing another.

This portion of the unit of study supports what will become complex work around characters and setting. As you demonstrate this work, the most important thing about the minilesson is that you are sharing your reading with your children. You are showing them that readers are alert to what they are doing as they read. The power of the minilesson will not reside in the specific lessons so much as in your willingness to notice and reflect on the mental work you do as you read. Your big message is that within this unit of study, you and your kids will not only rise to new challenges, but you will do so in the company of each other, aware that the complex books you'll all read together will require a lot of mental work and aware, too, that you'll be changed in the process of doing that work.

MINILESSON

Synthesizing Story Elements

CONNECTION

Tell children that you and your colleagues have also formed historical fiction book clubs. Invite children to join you in researching the mind work involved in this reading.

"Readers, yesterday when you formed reading clubs, I kept thinking about how similar this work is for you and for me. I'm not sure if you realize it, but the other teachers and I have formed a historical fiction book club, too. We were reading *The Book Thief*, which is set in Germany, right as the Nazis come to power. Yesterday, the other teachers and I spent some time just sitting alongside each other, reading. It was so quiet that you could hear the pages turn.

"After a few minutes, though, I broke the silence and asked everyone if maybe we could compare notes on the thinking that we were doing. We went around the table, trying to find the words to describe our thinking—and that was not easy. The amazing thing was that many of us had similar ways of describing the mind work we were doing.

"So I thought I'd tell you what *we* found ourselves doing as we began reading historical fiction, and ask if today, *you* might each spy on yourself as you read and see if you find yourself doing something similar. I'm hoping that in this way, we can almost be part of a shared research project. It could be that we, at this school, might uncover the secrets to how skilled readers approach historical fiction books."

Name your teaching point. Specifically, tell children that some readers of historical fiction begin a book collecting and noting the elements of story as we encounter them.

COACHING TIPS

In this minilesson, I aim to tell children about the mind work that my colleagues and I found ourselves doing as we read. Notice that I could have cut to the chase and just told them what I think I do as I read historical fiction. Instead, I embed those insights into what is a Small Moment story, a personal narrative, in which I proceed, step by step, along through the sequence of events that prompted us to make these realizations. I do this because I'm trying to draw kids in to what I'm hoping to communicate, and this is one way to do so.

"Specifically, I want to teach you that when the grown-ups in my book club and I began reading our historical fiction books, we found ourselves almost tacking up information we'd need to know on mental bulletin boards. At the start of our books, there was so much information flying past us as we read that we felt as if a lot of our mind work was spent catching the important stuff and almost sorting it so that we began to grasp the who, what, where, when, and why of the book."

TEACHING

Tell children that when you began your historical fiction book, instead of being lost in the story, you found yourself taking note of the fast-flying information and then returning to your notes to fill in details.

"We expected that as we began reading these books, we'd find ourselves lost in the story, dreaming the dream of the story, envisioning it. Maybe some of you will do that right away. But for most of us, it felt as if, at the very beginning of historical fiction books, there were too many vital statistics for us to take in, so rather than sliding into a dreamy state, we needed to be extra alert and focused on getting the information straight. We couldn't let ourselves go so fast that we were lost in the story and flying through it, at least not at the start of these books. Instead, it almost seemed as if we were taking mental notes as we read, rapidly trying to gather in all the essentials before something new came at us.

"We'd meet a character and tack that character up on a mental bulletin board, and then we'd meet another and do the same. We'd read on and find ourselves coming back to fill in a few details about the first character and the next one. We'd learn the place in which the story was set, and that information would go up on our mental bulletin boards. Later, we'd fill in details about that place. We learned the era, too, and tacked that up as well.

You may want to change the analogy to one that better suits your class. For example, instead of saying "mental bulletin board," you might try saying "the white board in your brain" or "a mental list." It goes without saying that you can alter any minilesson so that you use the words that fit you to a T. Perhaps, for you, reading historical fiction, or complex stories, is more like constructing a house, starting a blog, organizing a stamp collection. Really, truly, what matters most is that you convey something like this to kids: "Like you, I've been reading historical fiction and oh my, so much goes on in my mind as I read. It's unbelievable. I know the same will be true for you. So let's go to it. And later, the great thing is, we'll be able to gather with our friends and put this amazing intense experience into words."

Whatever words you use, make sure they resonate with children so they understand that the work you do as a reader of these complex texts involves locating, holding onto, and making sense of the fast-flying information readers encounter when starting a new book.

Throughout this series, you'll notice that I tend to use lots of words to describe what I and others do when we read. I am convinced that this is part of being explicit and transparent. I do not think it is enough to say to children, "As I read, I determine importance, infer, and synthesize." Instead, I think we need to turn the technical jargon of the profession into straight talk. This will help kids, but it will also help the profession because I think far too many of us assume we all know what these code words mean, and that we all know what is entailed in any one of these reading skills, while the truth of the matter is that if we all pulled chairs alongside a young reader and watched that reader at work, the youngster would have a thought, and one of us would say, "That's synthesis," and another, "That's inference," and still others would identify the work as yet other skills.

"I have come to believe that when reading historical fiction—and indeed, when reading many complex novels—there is so much information at the start of a book, and frankly throughout the book, that a good deal of our mind work needs to be spent catching the important stuff, pinning it onto a mental bulletin board, so that we grasp the who, what, where, when, and why of the book."

Set children up to research as you demonstrate this process of reading. Pause to scrawl important elements onto a piece of chart paper, keeping notes brief and in boxes-and-bullets format.

"Let me show you what I mean. It is time to start a new book, and we're going to be reading one of the most gorgeous historical fiction books of all time: *Number the Stars*, by Lois Lowry. Thousands of readers have read and talked about this book. It has been translated into many languages, so we'll be joining a global community that is connected through this story. Like so many historical fiction books, *Number the Stars* will be hard to put down.

"For now, I'm going to read just a bit and show you what I mean when I say that as I read, I find myself tacking things up on my mental bulletin board. As I do this, I want you to do similar note-taking alongside me, and after a bit I'll stop jotting and ask you to continue without me."

You'll notice that I do not record these terms onto chart paper or make an enormous point out of them. I don't do this because the key concept I am trying to convey is not that there is something critical about each of those questions. Instead, I'm using them as "for instances" to help kids understand that I'm trying to get a grip on the vital facts of the story, on the essential story elements.

You'll want to take note of the pace at which we read this beautiful book. You may recall that when working with The Tiger Rising, we crept through the first third of the book, returning to a few sections repeatedly, and then read the final half fairly quickly. The pace at which we read this book is not all that different. During the first portion of the book, there is a lot to discuss and lots of teaching potential to tap. Just be sure that you do not in any way expect that your children will creep through their historical fiction books in sync with your progress through this book! Keep in mind that some of them will be reading books that can be read in two or three days and that few will require more than a week of reading.

"I'll race you to the corner, Ellen!" Annemarie adjusted the thick leather pack on her back so that her schoolbooks balanced evenly. "Ready?" She looked at her best friend.

Ellen made a face. "No," she said, laughing. "You know I can't beat you—my legs aren't as long. Can't we walk, like civilized people?" She was a stocky ten-year-old, unlike lanky Annemarie.

"So let's stop there." Turning to the board, I muttered to myself, "What am I mentally noting?" Then I added, by way of explanation to the kids, "Usually I wouldn't *record* what's in my mind, but for now, we'll put the notes we are making in our mind out into the world." I jotted on the board:

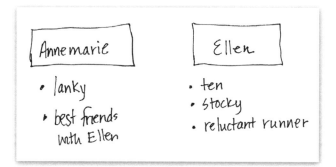

Then I resumed reading, repeating just a line.

. . . She was a stocky ten-year-old, unlike lanky Annemarie.

"We have to practice for the athletic meet on Friday—I *know* I'm going to win the girls' race this week. I was second last week, but I've been practicing every day. Come on, Ellen," Annemarie pleaded, eyeing the distance to the next corner of the Copenhagen street. "Please?"

After reading this scores of times, it just occurred to me that Bridge to Terabithia *and* Maniac Magee *and* Number the Stars *all start with children running in a race. How interesting! And how interesting that I never noticed this before now. I'm reminded constantly of the value of rereading and the fact that readers don't do this enough.*

There are so many teaching decisions that one needs to make all the time. Do you want to describe Annemarie as "lanky" or to paraphrase as "tall and thin." If you choose lanky *and think your children can't deduce the meaning of the word, you might mutter to yourself, as you write the descriptor, "I love this word. Lois Lowry could have said that she was tall and thin, but* lanky *says so much more, doesn't it? I picture her as gangling, like Abe Lincoln."*

Ellen hesitated, then nodded and shifted her own rucksack of books against her shoulders. "Oh, all right. Ready," she said.

I again gestured for children to add to their notes, and meanwhile I did so as well, adding the word "Copenhagen" and beside it, in parentheses, "Denmark." I also added to my notes on the two characters.

You may ask, 'Isn't this really active involvement? And the question would reflect a lot of wisdom. What I hope you come to realize is that the line between effective demonstrations and scaffolded practice is always a very thin one. While the teacher demonstrates, we ideally hope that kids are doing the work alongside us. And often, what happens in one section of a minilesson and another is interchangeable.

Process what you have done in ways that are transferable to another day, another text. Highlight the boxes-and-bullets format of notes, your attention to setting and characters, and the fact that notes reflect decisions about importance.

Then I paused and said to the children, "Do you see that I take notes in what is almost a boxes-and-bullets form? I record the main ideas or topics—a character's name, for example—and then I'll later return to that name and under it, jot some details. Annemarie is blonde, tall, a good runner, best friends with Ellen, and perhaps she's prone to brag. I'll continue on in the story, but I want you to notice that the information I get in a later paragraph of the text is often added alongside a note recorded at the very start of my reading as I find new stuff that relates to something I noted earlier.

Boxes and bullets can as easily be used to describe the parts of a frog body as it can to tell about the reasons why someone is important and as it can now, in this example, describe details about a character in a complex story.

"The other thing I hope you notice is that when I read 'Copenhagen,' I recall what I know about the place. Had I not known anything about Copenhagen, I would have found it on the map. That's why I've put globes and maps near your reading places. Of course, as I read on, I'm going to expect to learn a lot more about the place, and the information will go on my mental bulletin board."

Notice that I've tucked little tips into this teaching. You should be able to reread any teaching section of any minilesson, noting a handful of precise little tips embedded into the teaching. Sometimes teachers erroneously think that the teaching point encapsulates every bit of teaching contained in a minilesson, but if that were the case, there'd be no reason for people to listen past the statement of the teaching point.

ACTIVE INVOLVEMENT

Continue reading aloud, asking children to record vital information as they listen in preparation for sharing with club-mates.

"While I read, add to your mental (and physical) bulletin board. Later, you and your club mates can compare notes, seeing if you took note of similar things. [Fig. III-1]

> "Go!" shouted Annemarie, and the two girls were off, racing along the residential sidewalk. Annemarie's silvery blond hair flew behind her, and Ellen's dark pigtails bounced against her shoulders.
>
> "Wait for me!" wailed little Kirsti, left behind, but the two older girls weren't listening.
>
> Annemarie outdistanced her friend quickly, even though one of her shoes came untied as she sped along the street called Osterbrogade, past the small shops and cafes of her neighborhood here in northeast Copenhagen. Laughing, she skirted an elderly lady in black who carried a shopping bag made of string. A young woman pushing a baby in a carriage moved aside to make way. The corner was just ahead.

Channel children to talk with club-mates, thinking about whether differences between their notes reflect varying views on what seems to be important.

"Readers, I can see you've been jotting. Compare and combine your notes.

You'll want to think about the details of what you ask children to do. Where are they doing this note-taking? In their reading notebooks? On Post-its that they'll put on a sheet in their club folder? In one child's notebook that will be set at the center of where the club members are all sitting?

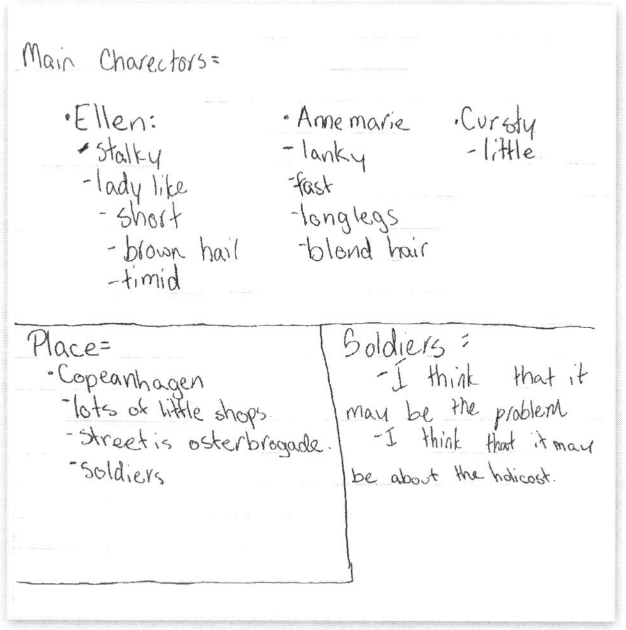

Figure III-1

One of the interesting things to note is that my instructions are more focused than usual. I have not simply said, "Turn and talk." I've used the academic vocabulary: "Compare and combine your notes." It is worth noting that of any academic vocabulary words, the most important words for children to understand are those used to describe what learners do. It is important for kids to grow into an understanding of terms such as contrast, summarize, analyze, list factors, and cite conditions. Some researchers suggest that all the teachers in a school might work to be sure their use of these terms is in sync and to be sure they use them often. "Turn and talk" can then become "turn and summarize" or "turn and list factors that caused. . . ." This, of course, would only be powerful if we then held children to actually doing that work.

Children began talking in their clubs, and I circulated from one group to another. In many clubs, youngsters simply presented what they'd written in a round-robin fashion. After a minute, I intervened. "Readers, can I have your eyes?" After I had their attention, I continued, "Let me remind you that I didn't suggest, 'Stop and read what you wrote to each other.' Instead, I lifted the complexity of my instructions. Listen again to them: 'Stop and *compare* your notes and combine them.' How are your ideas about the characters in your story different than the ideas that others had? Right now, just look at your notes and at the notes of the person next to you and don't say anything. Just get some thoughts in your minds." After children got started working, I voiced over a quiet reminder: "Let's turn and—listen carefully—compare and combine. After you have compared, combine your notes so you have a list of words or ideas for each of the main characters."

If you are teaching really sophisticated readers, you could elaborate on the meta-cognitive work you've asked readers to do, saying, "It is so fascinating, isn't it, to notice times when you recorded and valued details that others thought aren't important. If you see differences like that, you will want to explore the reasons behind them. One of the real challenges in reading is a skill called 'determining importance.' So if one person thinks it matters that Ellen has brown hair and Annemarie is blonde and thinks those details should be recorded, and others think those details aren't important, you'll want to debate that. If you want to look back on the page we read, signal to me, and I'll give you a copy so you can reference it. Continue working." You could later point out to children, "We won't actually know for certain whether the character's hair color, for example, will turn out to be important until we read on, but skilled readers do not pay equal attention to everything. When we read with a club, we can talk through reasons for thinking something might turn out to be important." But this aside might fly over the heads of many third graders.

Resume reading aloud, asking readers to take mental notes only, pointing to the place in their notes where they would have recorded a new detail had they been writing. Explain that as stories pick up speed, readers put down physical but not mental pens.

If you are thinking that this portion of the minilesson could easily be saved for tomorrow, you are right. You'll decide based on your assessment of your class and based, too, on whether you want kids to take note (physically, on the page) for an entire day before releasing them from that charge (as I suggest doing here). The work you have just asked youngsters to do—note-taking and then discussing differences in those notes and using that to discuss what seems to be more and less important in the text—is definitely work that children could be doing today as readers and as club-mates. If you decide to do so, you can easily diverge from my sequence, which instead moves readers to take notes in their minds only.

Another alternative is that the upcoming instruction could be the mid-workshop teaching point.

"I'm going to continue reading, but let me point out that when we read, we take some notes *in our minds* only. Usually the things we jot onto paper are either especially important or especially confusing. We record stuff we want to think about more. So as I read on, if you hear something about a character that does not seem important to ponder, then take note *in your mind* only. For now, so I can see your mind work, do this by literally pointing to the place in your notes where you mentally (but not actu-

Again and again, you'll see opportunities where you might decide to teach differently. If it is a real challenge to mobilize children, and you do not want to give children an out from taking notes just yet, then you can, of course, decide to not invite them to vary their reading based on what the text seems to want them to do.

ally) jot a note. That is, if you learn about the place, but it doesn't seem important to record, then take note in your mind, but point to the spot in your notes where you *could* record that. If the detail seems worth pondering, then record it."

Point out that the author gives readers signals for how to read a text.

"The other thing I want to tell you is that as you read, you are following the signals that the author gives you. Sometimes the author will signal that this section of the text contains lots of vital statistics and you must take note of tons of stuff. But sometimes, the story will pick up its pace, almost as if the author says, 'Put down your pencil and read, read, read. This is an exciting part.'"

Set children up to try the work you just demonstrated, taking mental notes either about important information in the story or about parts they wish to return to later, and putting their pencils down during parts the author signals them to read quickly.

You may have decided to not discuss the option of mental note-taking, in which case you may ask everyone to read, tacking up important information on a metaphoric bulletin board. In any case, presumably, you'll expect your kids to note-take either on a page in their reading notebooks or on Post-its that they'll contribute to a page on a timeline that can be placed at the center of the club's meeting place. If club members can all contribute to one big record of the story, adding details underneath each other's jottings, you'll find that kids will be especially engaged. They'll also benefit from looking across each other's notes every time they gather. You'll see that if kids maintain one central note-taking place, then as kids read, when one records something, others will look up from their reading and literally take note. The down side of a decision to support collaborative note-taking is that it does not set the clubs up to talk about the different decisions club members make, each on his or her own, about what merits being recorded. But there are pluses and minuses to every decision.

"You ready? Listen and follow the author's lead, taking written notes perhaps about the who, what, when, why, and where of this story, or about details you want to rethink later. You may find that this is a passage in which the author signals for you to just read, read, read, in which case—pencils (I held an imaginary pencil) down (I let go of it)."

Your students may already be using much of what you taught in your first two sessions, which means they'll be alert for setting details that they may have otherwise missed. They'll certainly be more alert to atmosphere. For instance, they'll probably be alert to how Annemarie's town is becoming frightening, just as Rose Blanche's did. They may jot the presence of Nazi soldiers, or they may just make a mental note of it. Some may remember the soldiers winking at Rose Blanche, whereas these soldiers glare at Annemarie.

Pick up your pace and get lost in this section of the text. You expect that soon kids will put down their imaginary pencils.

Annemarie . . . sped along the street called Osterbrogade, past the small shops and cafés of her neighborhood here in northeast Copenhagen. (You expect many kids will be pointing to their notes where they have recorded the place.) Laughing, she skirted an elderly lady in black who carried a shopping bag made of string. A young woman pushing a baby in a carriage moved aside to make way. The corner was just ahead.

Annemarie looked up, panting, just as she reached the corner. Her laughter stopped. Her heart seemed to skip a beat.

"Halte!" the soldier ordered in a stern voice.

The German word was as familiar as it was frightening. Annemarie had heard it often enough before, but it had never been directed to her until now.

Behind her, Ellen also slowed and stopped. Far back, little Kirsti was plodding along, her face in a pout because the girls hadn't waited for her.

Annemarie stared up. There were two of them. That meant two helmets, two sets of cold eyes glaring at her, and four shiny tall boots planted firmly on the sidewalk, blocking her path to home.

And it meant two rifles in the hands of the soldiers. She stared at the rifles first. Then, finally, she looked into the face of the soldier who had ordered her to halt.

"Why are you running?" the harsh voice asked. His Danish was very poor. Three years, Annemarie thought with contempt. Three years they've been in our country and still they can't speak our language.

"I was racing with my friend," she answered politely. "We have races at school every Friday, and I want to do well, so I—" Her voice trailed away, the sentence unfinished. Don't talk so much, she told herself. Just answer them, that's all.

She glanced back. Ellen was motionless on the sidewalk, a few yards behind her. Farther back, Kirsti was still sulking, and walking slowly toward the corner. Nearby, a woman had come to the doorway of a shop and was standing, silently, watching.

One of the soldiers, the taller one, moved toward her. Annemarie recognized him as the one she and Ellen always called, in whispers, "the Giraffe" because of his height and the long neck that extended from his stiff collar.

You'll not have time to notice some of the details of the scene right now. For example, one of the things that is important in historical fiction and, indeed, in most books that are level R and beyond, is that the setting tends to exert a force in the story. The setting is not just a place—school, the zoo—it is an event. Things happen in the setting; the setting changes. In historical fiction, events in history enter into and affect the plotline of the story, and indeed, you could say that much of the story revolves around the different characters' different responses to events in history. In this instance, the German soldiers intrude into the plotline of the main character, calling "Halte!" And it is telling to see the varied responses that the different characters have to this event. As you read on, you'll read about Ellen's mother's response to the event, and that becomes part of the story.

Here, your reading might change a bit. They are out of danger. There are facts in this section that might be noted mentally, though probably not physically.

Deconstruct what children just did, complimenting them on a job well done.

"I loved watching how some of you did some quick jottings as you learned that there are soldiers in this town now. And then I saw that many of you put down your mental (and real) pencils so you could read, read, read. You were worried for the girls. Toward the end, some of you jotted notes about the individual soldiers, which is wise, because they are new characters and we learned a few facts about them."

LINK

Send children off to read, expecting club mates will sit near each other and asking them to note important information unless their club's book is written in such a way that it channels them to put note-taking aside, getting lost in the story.

"So today, readers, we will read for thirty minutes, and then we'll meet in clubs for ten minutes. A few of you will be starting your second or maybe even your third book. For those of you who are beginning a book, I hope you notice whether you are almost tacking up information you need to know on mental bulletin boards. If your book is written in a way that seems to nudge you to take notes, as we found was true for the first two pages of *Number the Stars*, actually jot your notes on a page of your reading notebook so that you and your club mates can again talk about the different decisions you make about how to organize those notes and about what seems important to note. You won't be recording notes about facts forever. It's a way to get a book started. I'm doing the same with my club. *[Fig. III-2]*

"Meanwhile, though, parts of your book may be written like that breathtaking page we just read in *Number the Stars*. The author may seem to be saying, 'Put down your pencils and read, read, read,' and if that is so, your job is to be the kind of reader that is required by this book, at this part. You'll be a different kind of reader in different sections of your book, and when your club meets, you'll compare notes on that.

"Remember to fill in your logs and to read just to the point in the text that your club has set as your goalpost. If you get there early, you will need another book on deck. Don't read past your goalpost, or you'll lose track of what you were noticing and thinking."

Some historical fiction texts begin almost as one might expect children's realistic fiction to start—with someone in the midst of some action, and with the plotline as the dominant force in the story. Those historical fiction stories only bring out the setting and the context after the readers have grabbed onto the story line. Yet in other historical fiction books, the opening pages are devoted to building the context, to laying out the characters. I'm hoping that today's invitation is broad and flexible enough that readers can read their books responsively, doing the work the texts nudge them to do.

Figure III-2

CONFERRING AND SMALL-GROUP WORK

Coach Club Members to Rehearse for Conversations About Story Elements

During most of the previous units of study, the mid-workshop teaching point was inserted into reading time, with the share session setting up and bringing closure to partnership work at the end of reading time. Now that the reading workshop will sometimes include club meetings and sometimes won't, the mid-workshop teaching point will be used in more flexible ways. Sometimes this will come after half an hour of reading and will be a voiceover, coaching into children's reading work, and sometimes, like on this day, it will come after half an hour and will launch clubs, marking the transition between independent reading and book club work.

MID-WORKSHOP TEACHING POINT (TO LAUNCH CLUBS)

Readers Create Shared Goals with Club Mates

"Readers," I said. "In a minute, you'll have a chance to meet with your club-mates, and you'll talk over the thinking you have found yourself doing thus far in your book. Let me ask you some questions to get you ready to talk with each other. I talked today, and two days ago, too, about the thinking that the other teachers and I have been doing as we started historical fiction books. What has been going on in *your* mind as you read today? Did you find yourself immersed in the world of your story, alert to the tone, atmosphere, and tension of the world in which the story is set? Or were you tacking bits of information up on your mental bulletin board, trying to get your mental arms around the facts of the story?"

I left a pool of silence and then asked another set of questions. "What do you think would be worth talking about with your reading club-mates? What have you recorded? You should have a few topics in mind that are generally talk-worthy. Let me suggest a couple of these, and then you and your club-mates can decide if you want to talk about these:

- Any story is built around a main character who has traits, motivations, and problems, and as you get into challenging books, you'll come to know characters who, like Rob and Sistine, are layered and complicated.
- In historical fiction stories, the characters often face pressures, and things happen in the world that are challenging for them.
- The places in your story will be important, and you'll want to think not just about the physical attributes of those places but also the atmosphere, the feelings.

"I've written some of the things readers tend to do early on in a book, especially historical fiction. We're going to be adding to this chart throughout this unit, spotlighting what readers do as we make our way through our historical fiction texts.

"As you talk, try to keep some sort of written record at the center of the conversation, so use notes to ground your conversation. Be sure, though, that you remember that notes are meant as abbreviations. You write just a word, a phrase, and try to talk long and deep about the little tiny bit that you fasten onto the page."

Making Our Way Through Historical Fiction

- Collect setting details. What kind of place is this? What does it feel like?

- Is trouble brewing? How is it changing? What feels important?

- Collect vital data about characters. Traits? Pressures on them? Problems they face? What drives them?

Conferring and Small-Group Work

For these first few days, when children have just begun meeting in clubs, you and I once again will feel like those circus men who run around trying to keep plates spinning on the ends of sticks.

You'll need to move quickly among them, trying, with just a light touch, to keep kids productively engaged. This means that one goal for now will be to help readers carry on in less than perfect ways but with independence and engagement. But ultimately, the way to keep members of a club engaged is to help that club fashion a direction for itself and adopt shared goals, and you can't do this work until you have taken a tiny bit of time for assessment.

You've set children up to talk in important ways about the characters and the settings in their historical fiction novels and channeled them to create club notes of some sort—probably in the form of boxes and bullets on the characters and the places. Within a day, you'll help them jot notes in the form of several parallel timelines that capture the unfolding sequence of the story. There are enough optional ways to use club time that are in the air today to enable you to spend some of your teaching time thinking about the needs of readers in one club in contrast to another club.

Adding assessment to your responsibilities may well feel as if you are changing the tire on your car while driving seventy mph down the highway—but nevertheless, it is important to do. And actually, if you prepare your own mind to assess, the real-time work is not as extensive as you'd think, because you'll essentially be watching and listening with special alertness while you meanwhile handle all the other challenges that will be coming your way.

You Control Your Governing Gaze

Right now, as you read this, imagine yourself drawing a chair alongside one of your book clubs while the kids are in the midst of a conversation about their books, and imagine yourself recording whatever comes to your mind as you assess those youngsters. After jotting a few notes down, in your mind, travel to a second club and do the same thing. Actually take the time to do this in your mind's eye. If you actually do this, I'll be able to show you something. So come on, imagine yourself watching one of your book clubs. What will you see the kids doing?

Here is my point. My colleagues and I at the Teachers College Reading and Writing Project have worked with literally thousands of teachers, and we've found that it is almost invariably the case that if a teacher observes children talking in clubs about a shared book, the teacher will notice kids' abilities to talk and perhaps to write about reading. People leave such observations of book clubs with a list of skills that could be taught, *and all these skills are related to talk*. I've discussed those skills in the previous session—they *are* important and teachable—but for now, my point is that it probably won't be second nature for you to observe a book talk and come away with a sense for the *reading* work (not the talk work) that kids are or are not yet doing. Unless you consciously work against the tendency to keep your governing gaze steadily on children's abilities to talk well together and you deliberately attend to the reading skills and habits that are and are not revealed through that talk and through other signs, you won't see that this child is starting to synthesize sections from earlier in the text as he reads later related sections, but that the synthesis work has somehow led him to also merge all the different characters' perspectives into one—that he shows no awareness yet of the multiple perspectives held by different characters within the book. You will instead see that the members of this club are talking on top of each other or saying the same things over and over or talking in disjointed ways that make it hard for the club members to get onto a line of discussion. These are important things to see, but they need to be just part of your visual landscape.

The good news is that you and I can take ourselves firmly in hand, issuing executive orders to ourselves. "Lucy," I can say to myself, "as you observe book conversations today, listen for evidence that kids are almost or are actually using *reading* (not just talk) skills, and listen to see how they use those comprehension skills to notice more in what they are reading. Look especially for those whose command of a skill seems more developed and the ways in which that is so."

This means that if I pull a chair alongside a book conversation and hear Emma say, "It was so mean of Rifka's family to leave her all alone in Belgium, just 'cause she had ringworm, and for them to go to America without her. I mean she was–" And I see Izzy then butt in rudely, cutting Emma off to say, "But fifteen-year-olds were going into the Army in those days, and they sent her loads of money which was almost impossible to get then and–" Whereupon Emma continues, talking on top of Izzy, saying, "My mother would never leave me 'cause I was sick. Rifka's mother doesn't care. . . ." I can see the children's work as an example of readers not giving each other time to finish what they were saying—and it is—or I could see it as evidence that Izzy is not only imagining the world of the story but also viewing her characters through the perspective of that time and place, and that Emma's tendency to empathize is getting in the way of her being able to think of characters from within the perspective of their context.

There are concrete things we can do that will help us to see the kids' discussions as evidence of their reading work. Think of it this way. If you want to walk in the woods, thinking about the colors of the woods, it might help to walk with a painter at your side, or to bring a palette of paints with you into the woods. If you want to take that same walk thinking about kinds of trees, it would help to bring a field guide to trees with you, and even to have taken a few moments to review the predominate kinds of trees that are apt to be in your woods. In a similar fashion, you and I can take specific actions to help us see with the lens we choose to bring with us.

You Can Assess Readers' Comprehension Skills

Because I know that although the kids think of the upcoming unit as a unit on historical fiction but also that I am using historical fiction as a vehicle for teaching higher-level comprehension skills, I want to approach the unit keeping my readers' comprehension skills in the forefront of my mind. I'm interested in the skills I taught during our earlier fiction unit— the skills of envisionment, prediction, and growing theories about characters—because I want to see if readers have developed those skills while our focus was averted toward nonfiction reading. But I am also interested in the relationship between those skills and the challenge to read increasingly complex texts. Take envisionment. It will help if I pause to ask, "What sort of envisionment work will readers need to be doing now that they are reading historical fiction?' There may be many answers to that question, but right away I'm struck by the fact that it will be much harder for readers to draw on their own experiences when they envision and more essential that they read alert to textual clues that will help them envision the particulars of this story setting. If a character in a story set in Colonial America opens the door to her school and enters the building, the school won't look much like the schools that today's reader attends.

Envisioning surely is a critical skill for readers of historical fiction—and a much more difficult skill than it was when children tended to read realistic fiction. By thinking a bit about the challenges readers are apt to encounter with this skill and other skills, I'm more prepared to notice what they do as they read.

Before observing children's reading to assess it, I will also not only ask myself, "How will their prediction work change now that they are not only reading historical fiction but, more specifically, reading more complex fiction?" For starters, as readers progress from one band of text difficulty to another, the structure of stories will tend to become far more complex. Readers of N/O/P/Q texts will need to continue to construct a coherent overarching story line despite more side roads and subordinate anecdotes, and readers of texts that are R and above will need to take into account multiple plotlines, subordinate characters, and a changing setting that tends to influence the plot. So this means that if nothing else, one hopes that as readers move into texts of increasing complexity, they take more sources of information into account as they predict. For example, one hopes that a reader of an R/S/T text will notice the minor character that entered and left the scene early in the book and predict that perhaps that character might return to play a role later in the ensuing story line.

When I'm trying to prime my own thinking about reading skills so that I'm more apt to see the evidence of them as I work with readers, it helps me to take a few minutes to think about the skills that different bands of text difficulty require. For example, I know readers who are working in the R/S/T or U/V or W/Y bands of text difficulty are increasingly likely to encounter books in which there will be gaps in time (such as those created by flashbacks and flash-forwards), and I know that in the W/Y band, these jumps in time are often not tagged. There may be no explicit warning to the reader that time has just jumped forward or backward, leaving the reader to simply infer this. Texts in the U/V band of difficulty contain frequent flashbacks and backstories, but most of these are tagged, so the alert reader is given support. Knowing this means that as I scan over the books in those bands to try to see possible sources of confusion, I look for places where time jumps forward and backward. When I see readers grappling with confusion over the sequence of time, I'll guide some readers to be more alert to the ways an author can signify that time has just jumped forward or backward. Is the font different? Does the page layout communicate the passage of time?

The upcoming unit will especially address the skills of interpretation, critical reading, and synthesis, so this is also a good time to find a way to assess what children can do with those reading skills. It's hard to have time to insert special assessments into the complexity of one's teaching, but if possible, it is incredibly worthwhile to take even just thirty minutes to read aloud a short story, inserting a few prompts into it as we did earlier with *One Green Apple*, only this time the prompts will nudge readers to show what they can do in the way of synthesizing and interpreting, as well as predicting and envisioning. If, as one of your prompts, you ask children to respond in writing to "What do you think will happen next?" be sure that you follow that question with "What sources of information led you to make this prediction?" Ask the question "How does this part connect with earlier sections of the story?" at a part when a skilled reader would see the resonance. And then, at or near the end, ask, "What is this text really, really about? What message is the author trying to say?" As always, you'll want to sort the evidence of readers' thinking, the writing in response to these prompts, into piles and to use this exercise to help you clarify to yourself what it is that you hope children do when they are asked to predict, envision, synthesize, interpret, and so forth.

You Can Assess for Volume, Pace, and Fluency of Reading

It is impossible to overemphasize the importance of continuing to keep your eyes on the volume of reading that your readers do and their speed and fluency as readers and their engagement with the texts they are reading. I want to emphasize this especially because when children are reading shared books and these are books that you know well, it is tempting to get into the mind-set—so common especially in high school teachers of literature—that the goal is to be sure that readers see everything in this text that you see in it. The goal can be to make sure that no symbol gets past readers' eyes unheralded, no literary reference goes unseen. This vigilant effort to "teach the text" can—and often does—lead readers to creep through novels, doing just a tiny fraction of the reading that Gentry's

research has shown is essential for readers to do (something like six level M books a week, and one level R/T book a week). Your goal is to strengthen readers' muscles, to develop their skills, to whet their reading appetite, and to enrich their background of reading experiences. It is not to make sure that each of your readers has an encyclopedic knowledge of one particular book! Who really cares whether any one child knows the meaning of any one symbol in any one text? What does matter is that as your children continue reading, reading, reading, they make more of the texts that they read.

So absolutely, you will want to keep your eye on the volume of reading that your students are doing. You can assess volume not only by looking at the logs but also by simply doing spot checks during the time you are allotting to reading. Keep a list of your children at your side (or ask a student teacher or a paraprofessional to do this for you), and then, over a day or two, make a point of scanning the room at ten-minute intervals during reading time to check off the names of kids who are, at that second, engaged in eyes-on-print reading. For now, don't even attempt to evaluate the worthiness of their alternate activities: simply look for eyes-on-print reading, and do this multiple times across two days. The patterns will be revealing! Then again, you could simply take note of which children are actually eyes-on-print reading five minutes after you disperse them from the meeting area with the injunction, "Get started on your reading."

The powerful thing about assessments such as these is that you needn't wait until the end of the year to see whether you effect change. You can collect this data on one Monday, aspire to teach in ways that foster engagement in a volume of reading, and you can assess again a week later, expecting the data to show improvement.

If you see that volume and pace seem to be problems, don't waste a minute before researching what the underlying issue might be. Sometimes writing about reading swamps reading itself, in which case you may want to suggest that kids limit themselves to writing only quick jotted notes, or you may want to suggest that they read for long chunks and then write as a reflective move after doing that reading. Note whether readers who are not getting through a lot of books are reading appropriate books. How is their fluency?

Once You Assess, You Can Use Your Assessments to Give Children a Sense of Agency

As you conduct these assessments, be sure that you are looking for what it is that children can do—for evidence of their growth and of their strengths. Be on guard against the very human tendency to think of assessing as identifying student needs or figuring out next steps for teaching. You'll have worked with your children for a good portion of the school year by now, and you should be in a position to show each child tangible evidence that he or she has grown. "Look at how you've changed!" you can say. "Holy moly, you are on such a growth spurt as a reader. Your path is like a lunar rocket!" There is probably nothing you can do that will maximize your children's learning curve more than showing children the changes you have already seen in their abilities as readers and helping them to see themselves as readers on the move.

You'll want to look for indicators of children's strengths for other reasons as well. For one, you're going to want to be transparent with kids about the work that you believe they need to be doing as readers. Your clubs will be vastly more effective and more powerful if the members of a reading club have agreed that together, they're going to tackle a goal or two. I'll discuss this more in Session IV, but for now, let me say that you can recruit that sort of buy-in and sense of personal and group agency if you are able to talk to readers about the impressive progress they've already made as well as about the next steps you believe are in store for them.

Then again, once you identify strengths, you can capitalize on them, helping children become mentors for each other. You can say to this individual or that one, "I'd really like for you to help others learn from your talent for. . . ." If, from your observations, you find yourself saying things such as, "The kids can't . . ." and "They're not good at . . . ," you won't have the ingredients you need to plan next steps. On the other hand, if you look for evidence that one member of a club is notably more adept at a skill that other club members need to develop, this will mean that there is a built-in mentor already on the ground in the club. You can then empower that embedded mentor, setting him or her up to help the others. Being called upon to do this will help the mentor, and meanwhile, a child embedded within a club will be able to provide other club members with more continual feedback than anything you could provide.

As you'll learn in greater detail in the upcoming sessions, because the reading workshop on most days will end with club time, and you will often give clubs leeway over how to use that time, the work that club members do when they convene will be shaped at least in part by the agenda they take on. For example, members of a club in which readers need to work on volume and fluency may decide to do a lot of reading aloud and reader's theater work within their club sessions. When you coach into that club's work, then, in addition to helping the club members with the work on the unit of study and with the challenge of talking well together, you'll help them with work such as noticing the tags that suggest that a character didn't just say some words, but yelled them or whispered them. Chances are good that those readers will be thrilled to take on roles as they read aloud and to add gestures to accompany the emotional sections of texts. Perhaps this club will want to establish a ritual of identifying a page that they'll discuss, and before discussing the page, asking someone from the club to read the page aloud. When you work with this club, you'll also want to devote more of your time to helping the club find books that they're dying to read. You can make any book worlds more interesting to young readers if you read aloud the first chapter or so and even return later to read another especially important chapter aloud.

Of course, these specific recommendations are not important. What is important is this: If you can rally members of a club to dedicate themselves to whatever the work is that you and the club decide is important, and if you can help the club members to invent some concrete ways of reaching that goal, then you will have tapped into the social energy in your classroom, using that energy to power growth in reading.

TEACHING SHARE

Readers Learn About the World Through Fiction

Demonstrate for your students how they can practice learning from fiction by retelling small bits of the story and then pausing to say what they have learned from that section.

"Readers, I've been listening to your book clubs. Your talk has reminded me to be sure you are noticing that as we read fiction, we learn tremendous amounts of real information—or we don't. Here's the secret. It's not hard to do. It's just really easy to *not* do! It's easy to be swept away by the plot, to just keep reading, devouring that book and moving on to the next book without really thinking about whether or not you've learned anything new.

"The brain is a muscle like any other muscle, and we can strengthen it. I practice learning from fiction by retelling parts of the story to myself in smallish bits, saying what happened in the story, and then pausing to insert something that I learned from that part of the story, something that I didn't know before.

"Watch me do this work. Listen for how I retell what happened in *Rose Blanche* and insert the new information I learned." I shifted my voice to signal I was musing. "Let's see, so the story started with Rose Blanche telling us about her town. Hmm, . . . , I *learned* that small towns in Germany sometimes had fountains and narrow streets and tall houses. I didn't know any of that. I've never been to Germany.

Then I said, in an aside. "Readers, did you hear how I inserted, '*I learned . . .*' and some facts? Let me go on. What happened next? Oh, yes, then the trucks started to come through, and then the tanks. Let me reread that part to you.

> They drive tanks that make sparks on the cobblestones. They are so
>
> noisy and smell like diesel oil. They hurt my ears.

Then I shifted to the thought prompt and said, "I learned . . . um . . . tanks make sparks when they drive on cobblestones. Tanks are loud and smell like diesel." Then I paused to look out at the class and to name what I'd just done. "Do you see that I retold small parts of the story, and then stopped to say what I learned after each part?"

COACHING TIPS

Here I position myself in the same place that so many eager young readers are. They are plot junkies. You are going to be asking your readers to slow down here, so that they take the time to accumulate new information.

Teachers, I explain how this kind of retelling is really an exercise because I want our readers to know that they will not always do this kind of slow, bit-by-bit examination of a story—or they would never get through their books. But when you are training yourself to do new work, you build up the muscles, isolating that muscle and developing exercises to train it. If you do Sudoku or play an instrument, you'll find you can develop this metaphor more powerfully. If you play a sport or dance or do something else where it's important to train yourself in certain actions so you can do them automatically, of course, delve into your personal history to use that as your metaphor.

It's the same way that an adult reader who reads Bel Canto *learns a lot about opera, or the reader of the* Guernsey Literary *and* Potato Peel Pie Society *finds out about the Channel Islands during World War II. Powerful readers come away from fiction stories with more information about the world.*

Ask your students to practice what you have demonstrated.

Then I said, "Will you and your club-mates practice this work? You can continue with *Rose Blanche*, or you can retell what has happened so far in your book, and then press yourself to say what you have learned related to social studies or history or science. Say, 'I've learned . . .' and then squeeze your mind to name some learning. I'll come around to listen."

Some children turned to their club books, extracting and accumulating information that had been embedded in earlier sections of it. *[Figs. III-3, III-4, and III-5]*

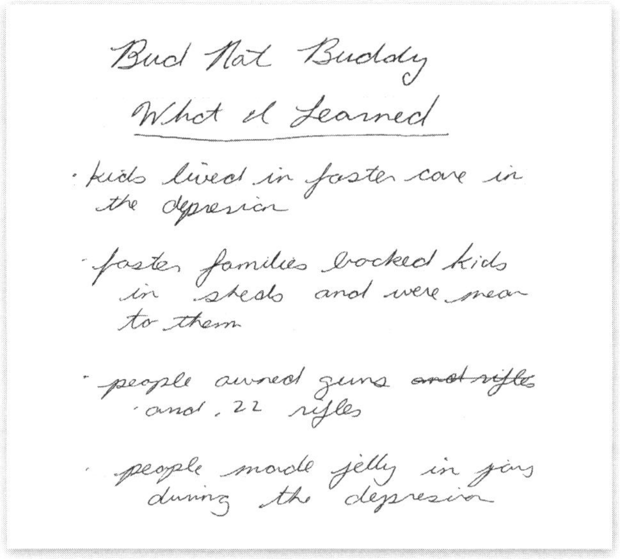
Bud Not Buddy

What I Learned

• kids lived in foster care in the depresion

• foster families locked kids in sheds and were mean to them

• people owned guns ~~and rifles~~ and .22 rifles

• people made jelly in jars during the depresion

Figure III-3

Of course, instead of turning children to their club books, I could have set them up to continue this work using the next section of Rose Blanche *as the practice text. It is probably more important, however, for readers to transfer this strategy to their books, and also to have as much time as possible talking with their club-mates.*

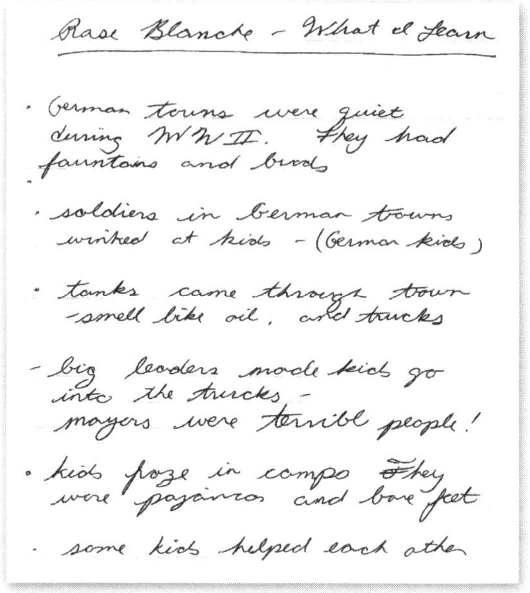
Rose Blanche – What I learn

• German towns were quiet during WWII. They had fountains and birds

• soldiers in German towns winked at kids – (German kids)

• tanks came through town – smell like oil, and trucks

– big leaders made kids go into the trucks – mayors were terrible people!

• kids froze in campo ~~They~~ wore pajamas and bare feet

• some kids helped each other

Figure III-4

Finally, I intervened to close the reading workshop. "Club members, time to stop. Be sure you have decided how many chapters you'll read tonight. In thirty minutes, you can read twenty-some pages, probably. And remember, each of you will need to keep a second book on hand so that you don't need to skimp on reading time, nor will you read past the page you decide upon. It is much more fun if you make a vow to not read past the page you decide upon together."

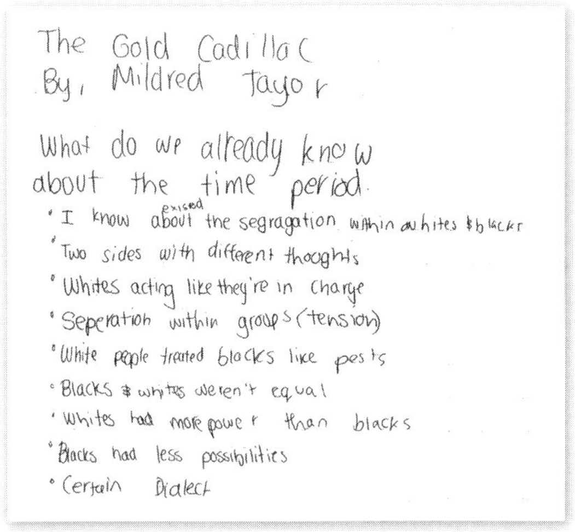

The Gold Cadillac
By, Mildred Taylor

What do we already know about the time period.
- I know about the segragation within whites & blacks
- Two sides with different thoughts
- Whites acting like they're in charge
- Seperation within groups (tension)
- White people treated blacks like pests
- Blacks & whites weren't equal
- Whites had more power than blacks
- Blacks had less possibilities
- Certain Dialect

Figure III-5

Holding On When Time Jumps Back and Forth

ou may glance at the title of this session and of the one that follows it and raise your eyebrows. You might ask, "Is it really necessary to devote so much time to basic story elements?" You might think, "Wasn't it months ago that we taught readers to construct timelines of their narratives?" And it is true that not only this session but this entire first part of the unit revisits skills that were taught earlier. You would be absolutely right to notice that this session harkens back to the retelling work from the very first unit of the year. But peek ahead at the minilesson and note the complexity of it; you'll be glimpsing not only the logic of this session but also the structure of these units of study.

A unit on historical fiction provides a perfect forum for teaching readers the skills of interpretation and critical reading, and it is tempting to want to move our teaching right to these high-level skills. Here's the thing, though. As the books that children read get more complicated, students need new teaching to help them comprehend the book. Essential comprehension work, even such work as keeping track of characters, needs new support. Just think about what it was like the first time you tried to read a Russian novel. Remember *Anna Karenina*? Remember desperately jotting the characters' names on the inside cover, drawing lines between those who were related? Remember keeping track of time and how it was passing, and who was even alive still?

It is critical to teach these comprehension essentials, helping students to understand the different ways that the stories they are reading are becoming more complicated: the multiple plotlines, the insertion of backstories, the characters who are not what they seem, the information the reader gets that is unavailable or opaque to the main character, the complicated emotional lives and motivations of characters,

GROWING POWERFUL BOOK CLUB CONVERSATIONS

- Make sure you have read the entire first chapter (only) of *Number the Stars* to your class before starting this minilesson.

- Select, and record on chart paper, short excerpts from this or another familiar text in which time does not unroll chronologically. You could use the excerpts from *Number the Stars* already spelled out in the active engagement.

- During the mid-workshop teaching point, you will need to be ready to add to the chart "Growing Powerful Book Club Conversations" chart.

- You'll need to have finished Chapter 2 in *Number the Stars* prior to teaching the next session, Session V.

the problems that remain unsolved. Disentangling these complexities is a critical part of deep comprehension. And here's the danger if we skip over this and rush toward work in interpretation: The kids become fancy talkers whose ideas emerge from the glossy surface of the story (or they become plot junkies who throw some themes around when required to do so). It is all too easy for kids to read only for what happens, noticing mostly the big events. They are not aware of the details that give this story a dense complexity. They both miss the richness of texts in the R/S/T band and are not

> *As the books that children read get more complicated, students need new teaching to help them comprehend the book.*

preparing to read texts above those levels, where almost all the story elements are ones you have to infer quickly from sparse information or very literary language. They may be eager to offer their ideas about stories, but those ideas are often based on extremely partial understandings of the story itself.

This session, then, will be one more in a progression of sessions that aims to help readers rise to the challenge of reading more complex texts. Specifically, the session will help readers understand that in complex novels, the sequence of events in the characters' lives and in history intersect. Events in the setting lead different characters to make different choices, to take different action, and all of this creates chains of action and reaction that form the bedrock of the story's plotline.

As readers progress toward reading increasingly complex books, the passage of time becomes more complex. Often significant events on the timelines of these stories happen before the story starts. The reader is told about them either through a monologue or through a conversation.

In books within the R/T and U/W bands of difficulty, if time jumps forward or backward, it will generally be well marked. The flashback or flash-forward might be prefaced with a phrase that cues the reader in or might be set off in italics or by a row of stars. Still, these passages will be challenging for young readers. Later, these changes aren't marked by text indicators, and they can happen rapidly. But early in the books, the more likely source of initial complexity will be the fact that much of what occurs in the first chapters of novels feels as if it is interrupted action. That is, implicit in the action at the start of many novels is a whole timeline of prior events.

The events in the backstory may be events from the character's prior life, or they may be events in the historical timeline. For example, in the first chapter of *Number the Stars*, readers learn a fair amount about prior events in history: The German soldiers have been in Copenhagen for three years, goods (including coffee) have been restricted during that time, some brave Danish resisters earlier exploded factories that could otherwise have been suppliers for the Nazis. Only later in this book do readers learn about the prior events in Annemarie's family—the death of the sister just before her wedding day, for example, and still later, what caused that death. That event, which happened in the past, before the story begins, keeps emerging within the story and is revealed across many pages and embedded within many future moments.

This session, then, highlights the work that readers need to do to construct a timeline as they read. The session helps youngsters be especially aware that complex novels often contain a backstory. It is worth noting that although this is a unit on reading historical fiction, the skills that you are teaching are skills that readers need to use when reading

any novel, and especially any complex novel. Reconsider the first few pages of *The Tiger Rising* using the lens of time, and you'll see how often the temporal lens shifts in that narration. That is, I encourage you to refrain from letting the focus on reading historical fiction sway you into thinking of these clubs as a forum for studying children's literature. You probably do not want to angle children's work so they spend a lot of time studying the characteristics of historical fiction, discussing which books do and do not fall within the genre specifications, or categorizing texts into different subgroups within the genre. Instead, you'll probably want to approach the unit thinking, "What are the challenges that more complex books pose for readers, and how can I help them rally to meet those challenges?"

Yesterday, in Session III, you shone a spotlight on the work readers need to do to synthesize information about characters and setting as they read. Today and tomorrow, you'll add one more element, reminding readers to also think about the sequence of time—both personal time and historical time. And of course, just because you address one element one day and another a second day, this doesn't mean that you expect readers to attend to these elements in isolation. Readers draw all sources of information together, on the run, as we move forward. And as readers tackle increasingly more complex texts, we're expected to draw on more sources of information, to keep more aspects of texts in mind as we read. Whereas when readers read books within the N/O/P/Q band of difficulty, there is usually one predominate story arc that binds together most of the story, with the protagonist entering the story with a overarching motivation, an enduring want, that in the end is resolved, when readers tackle more complex books, time does not march forward, and subordinate plotlines that are offstage for the reader (such as the backstory in *Number the Stars* of the dead sister, Lise, and her fiancé Peter) can end up play-

ing a major role in a story's resolution. In *Number the Stars*, for example, Lise's boyfriend, Peter, will resurface near the very end of the book to help safeguard the Rosens. The important thing about this is not that it occurs in this particular book but rather that your teaching needs to help readers keep more sources of information in mind as they read increasingly complex novels.

Tell kids the truth, which is that readers can read any book and be blind enough to nuance and complexity that they turn that text into a flat, plot-summary-like text. Eudora Welty once said, "Poetry is the school I went to to learn to write prose." As you enter this unit of study, you'll want to think, "Historical fiction will be the school my children go to to learn to tackle more complex texts."

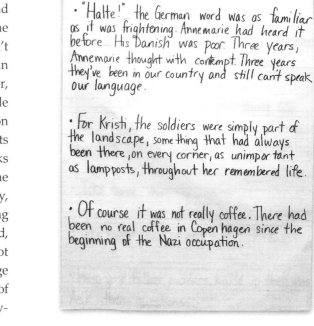

Passages From <u>Number the Stars</u>:

• "Halte!" the German word was as familiar as it was frightening. Annemarie had heard it before... His Danish was poor. Three years, Annemarie thought with contempt. Three years they've been in our country and still can't speak our language.

• For Kristi, the soldiers were simply part of the landscape, something that had always been there, on every corner, as unimportant as lampposts, throughout her remembered life.

• Of course it was not really coffee. There had been no real coffee in Copenhagen since the beginning of the Nazi occupation.

MINILESSON

Holding On When Time Jumps Back and Forth

CONNECTION

Remind readers that when starting to read a historical fiction book, or any book, we often "take note" of important story elements. Use a familiar, short text to demonstrate.

"Yesterday, we agreed that when we're starting a historical fiction book, there is often so much happening that for a bit, we need to sit up and take note of all incoming information. We especially need to tack the important story elements onto our mental bulletin boards.

"That sounds simple, and readers, it is simple when you are reading simple stories. When I read 'Jack and Jill went up the hill' to five-year-olds, for instance, I sometimes have a cutout figure of Jack, and as I read his name, I literally tack him onto the bulletin board to help us remember that so far, we have Jack. As I read Jill, I tack her beside Jack. Then I add the hill and the bucket of water at the top. When the poem says, 'Jack fell down and broke his crown,' I pick up the little figure of Jack and make him tumble head over heels.

"Here's the thing, though, readers. As your books get more complicated, what you notice and think about as you read also needs to get more complicated. Otherwise you could turn a story as complicated as *Rose Blanche* into something simple like Jack and Jill: Rose visits the camp on the edge of town. She gets shot and she falls down. It could sound like that, right? It would be a brutal nursery rhyme, but it would tell the simplest version of the story."

Notice that I'm providing graphic images to try to convey the mental work that readers can do. I think it is more helpful to talk about reading as "dreaming the dream of the story" rather than to use more technical terms such as "envisioning." But there are risks to using metaphors to capture what reading feels like. One of those is that our teaching can become swamped with so many lavish complex ways to represent a kind of mental work that children don't grasp instances when four different metaphors, in fact, are all efforts to talk about the same thing.

Of course when I describe the way I might read the nursery rhyme to five-year-olds, I act out everything as I say it. When I did this minilesson, I did not actually have a physical representation of Jack or of Jill, but still I pretended that I did. I pretended, too, that I had a bulletin board. Use every means possible to make your minilessons graphic. But in the end, pretending they are graphic works pretty well, too!

Emphasize that skilled readers don't take a rich book and reduce it to a simple straightforward nursery rhyme-like tale. Skilled readers see complexity.

"But here is the thing. Skilled readers don't take a complex story and turn it into something rather like 'Jack and Jill Went Up the Hill. Skilled readers notice complexities. We notice that characters are not just one way (we learned about that earlier in the year) and that characters sometimes act differently than they feel. We notice things about the characters that the author never comes straight out and says. We notice the relationship the character has with that place and how the place changes. Yesterday some of you noticed that Annemarie and Ellen seem almost like opposites. You noticed that the older children seem much more aware of their world than young, naive Kirsti. You didn't make the story into 'Annemarie and Ellen ran up the street. They saw a man standing on the corner.'

"You not only gathered all the incoming information, you jotted, you assembled your thinking, you put details together. You essentially are coauthoring this text, building your own understandings inside of and alongside the author's words, in the company of your reading friends. Just as good writers *write* with details, good readers *read* with details, with complexities. And I saw many of you doing that yesterday. Congratulations."

Name your teaching point. Teach children that skilled readers are aware that in complicated stories, time does not unroll evenly, and they are alert for signals about where they are in time, in the text.

"Today I want to teach you that when skilled readers read any complex story, and especially when we read historical fiction, we are aware that *time* is one of the elements in the story that is often complex. Specifically, we are aware that the spotlight of the story is not continually on the here and now. Sometimes the story harkens back to events that have already occurred, earlier in the story or even before the story began."

Of course this list could be longer and you'll vary it based on what your readers do already notice. If they are skilled, you could say, "We notice perspectives—and the way different perspectives reveal different aspects of the story." But you wouldn't add that to a summary if, in fact, your readers don't tend to notice this.

You could also point out that some readers noticed that Lois Lowry is playing into stereotypes when she suggests that Ellen, who is Jewish, has dark hair, doesn't run quickly, and is an amazing student. It would sound like: "Some of you noticed that the characters seem to fulfill stereotypes of being Jewish, or Aryan, by being dark and bookish, or blond and athletic." But this may be lost on your kids, so you may decide to reserve this for later.

Teaching

Illustrate the complexity of time by telling an adapted version of the same nursery rhyme, now including a backstory. Set children up to struggle to unravel the complex timeline of the adapted nursery rhyme.

"Let me show you what I mean when I say that sometimes time is represented in complex ways. Let's pretend each of us has a bulletin board in front of us (really it can be a sheet of paper), and as we read this little story, let's each record the main events in this story, as they occur on a timeline." Then I read this aloud, pausing for a few seconds at intervals to nudge people to make some quick efforts to capture the story line on paper.

> "Jack and Jill—who are the brother and sister who moved in right next door three years ago, on the day after their father left on a journey to a far land, who had a fierce dog that appeared on the same day their father departed, who fought every day and about everything so that for years they could never do anything together, who were kicked out of school a year ago and now have to be home schooled from their house—well, *yesterday* they went up a hill together to fetch a pail of water.

> "(Their mother, who has worked from home with a catering service since their father went on his journey, decided last week that she was tired of their fighting, so she ordered them to do all their chores together. One of the chores is to fetch water for the dog.) Anyhow, they were fetching the pail of water when Jack fell down and broke his crown and Jill came tumbling after. Now they're both in the hospital. Next weekend we can visit them, and while we're there, maybe we can hear more about whether the two of them have resolved their struggles, and what the mother did to help that to happen. Also about how, since the kids are in the hospital, the dog is fetching his own water."

Channel children to talk about the difficulties encountered trying to capture the sequence of a narrative that contains a lot of backstory.

"I bet it was not easy to capture on the page exactly what transpired in what time sequence! Talk in your clubs about what this was like for you."

The children buzzed for a minute, all saying that the story kept referencing events that happened prior to the main story line. If they recorded things in the order in which they heard of them, that would not be the order in which they occurred.

This is a complex text, and you'll want to be sure you read it in ways that help the kids grasp the meaning. Read it to yourself first and make sure you follow it! You'll need to read it fairly quickly, with your voice tucking little asides in as you pause the main story line to convey some explanatory information. As you read this aloud, don't even try to figure out what story sequence you expect your kids will reconstruct. The whole point will simply be that time can unroll in confusing ways.

Invite one child to reread the adapted nursery rhyme while you demonstrate how you go about sorting out the sequence of events within and before the story's present.

I gathered them back. "I'm going to ask Sam to reread the story, and let's work together to try to capture the sequence of events as they occurred in time in the world of the story. To do this, I want you to realize that we need to expect that as the story on the page unrolls, sometimes we, as readers, need to loop our minds backward." (I threw my arm over my shoulder, much as I'd done during Session XII of Unit 1.) "Sometimes as we read, we're not following the forward-moving story, but are instead filling in the backstory. A backstory is when you are told about things that happened before the story opens."

Sam read:

> "Jack and Jill—who are the brother and sister who moved in right next door three years ago, on the day after their father left on a journey to a far land, who had a fierce dog that appeared on the same day their father departed, who fought every day and about everything so that for years they could never do anything together, who were kicked out of school a year ago and now have to be home schooled from their house—well, *yesterday* they went up a hill together to fetch a pail of water."

"Let's start by recording the events in the main story line," I said, and recorded that Jack and Jill moved in.

"Now we need to start filling in the backstory, and it began three years ago." I added a few notes. My notes now listed that after Jack and Jill moved in their father left, but then I corrected myself.

"Oh, no! That happened before they moved in. The dog appeared. Okay, that's the same time that the father left." By this point, I had jotted:

> - Jack and Jill's father left and dog appeared
> - J + J moved in
> - J + J kicked out of school
> - J + J up hill for water

"Let's hear more of the story." I motioned for Sam to continue reading:

I asked Sam to do the honors because although all the words of this text are very straightforward, the text itself is extremely confusing. I felt it required a very facile reader.

"(Their mother, who has worked from home with a catering service since their father went on his journey, decided last week that she was tired of their fighting, so she ordered them to do all their chores together. One of the chores is to fetch water for the dog.) Anyhow, they were fetching the pail of water when Jack fell down and broke his crown and Jill came tumbling after. Now they're both in the hospital. Next weekend we can visit them, and while we're there, maybe we can hear more about whether the two of them have resolved their struggles, and what the mother did to help that to happen. Also about how, since the kids are in the hospital, the dog is fetching his own water."

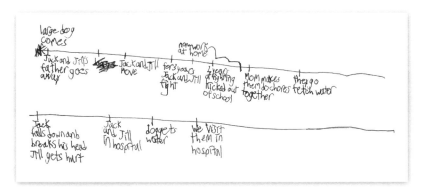

Figure IV-1

"We learned more about the events in the story line, didn't we?" I said. "Josh, may I show the class the timeline you have drawn?" Josh nodded, looking down with a little grin. [Fig. IV-1]

Name what it is that you have just demonstrated, emphasizing ways in which your work is transferable to another day and another text.

"This is not easy to do because, as one continues reading the story, sometimes you are learning what happens *next* and sometimes you are learning what happened *already*, before the actual start of the story action. I'm hoping that you are learning that when reading historical fiction, especially, but also any complex fiction, it helps to be aware that the passage of time will often not proceed sequentially. You'll be given backstories, like this one. Flashbacks happen when you go back in time and actually witness earlier events, often through the character's daydreams and nightmares. Sometimes there is foreshadowing, where the author tells how a day will end, before it even happens, like, 'he didn't know that he would never see his mother after today.'"

ACTIVE INVOLVEMENT

Set children up to wrestle with complex treatment of time by rereading tiny excerpts from the read-aloud text the class recently heard, selecting excerpts in which time jumps around.

"Let's practice thinking about time right now by going back to the first chapter of *Number the Stars*. I'll read aloud sections in which time does not unroll chronologically. See if you can come up with a name for what's going on, time-wise. If we have the language we need to talk about time when it jumps around, we'll be more ready for the complexities that one finds in historical fiction." I revealed chart paper on which I'd written these excerpts and read them aloud.

> "Halte!" the soldier ordered in a stern voice.
>
> The German voice was as familiar as it was frightening. Annemarie had heard it often enough before, but it had never been directed at her until now.
>
> . . . "Why are you running?" The harsh voice asked. His Danish was very poor. Three years, Annemarie thought with contempt. Three years they've been in our country, and still they can't speak our language.
>
> "I was racing with a friend," she answered politely. "We have races at school every Friday, and I want to do well, so I—" Her voice trailed away, the sentence unfinished.
>
> . . . For Kirsti, the soldiers were just part of the landscape, something that had always been there, on every corner, as unimportant as lampposts, throughout her remembered life.

"Talk with your club-mates. Try to put into words what you are noticing about the passage of time in these segments of the story. Instead of just saying something simple like, 'Time jumps around,' try to talk in precise words about what you notice about the treatment of time.

"Readers, I'm going to listen as you tell your club-mates a little bit about what you have discovered.

They talked.

As you listen, perhaps a child will point out that many aspects of the girls' daily life make them recall how things used to be. The contrast between now and then is ever-present for them. Perhaps they'll point out that the Nazis have been there for three years, and that length of time feels different for Kirsti than for the older girls.

If you want to share additional excerpts, you might draw on either of the following:

> Of course it was not really coffee. There had been no real coffee in Copenhagen since the beginning of the Nazi occupation.
>
> "Did you read in the De Frie Danske about the bombings in Hillerod and Dorrebro?"
>
> Although she pretended to be absorbed in unpacking her schoolbooks, Annemarie listened, and she knew what her mother was referring to. De Frie Danske—The Free Danes—was an illegal newspaper; Peter Neilsen brought it to them occasionally, carefully folded and hidden among ordinary books and papers, and Mama always burned it after she and Papa had read it. But Annemarie heard Mama and Papa talk, sometimes at night, about the news they received that way.

"Readers, as you were talking, you said that sometimes you find out about something that happens all the time. The character lets you know that it is a regular occurrence. Like Kirsti is used to seeing black boots and Nazi soldiers. You also said that other times, you find out that something has happened before, but the main character has never seen it. It's an event that has been off of his or her radar. Like Annemarie hasn't seen the bombings in Hillerod, or what the Resistance has done. She has only heard about it."

LINK

Reiterate the big work that you've been channeling children to do thus far in the unit, recalling earlier teaching points and putting today's new teaching point into the context of that larger repertoire.

After a few minutes, I intervened. "Readers, we'll talk more about ways in which time unrolls in a story. For now, the important thing is that when you are reading, you sit up and take note, tacking the important story elements of the story and the information that you are learning onto your mental bulletin board. You already know that you can be extra alert to details about the setting, and you're becoming extremely adept at paying attention to characters. At the start of more complicated books, you also need to get the plotline straight, so it often helps to think, 'Who is doing what, where, and, as we learned today, *in what order*?' Often it helps to keep timelines as you read or a quick list of important events, in order.

"And remember: Skilled readers notice complexities. Just as you all have learned by now to notice that characters are not just one way, and you have learned to notice that there are things about the characters that the author doesn't come straight out and say, you can also notice that time jumps around in stories, and the author does not come right out and warn you to pay attention when this happens. Sometimes the story will refer to events that have already occurred, and as an alert reader, you are supposed to pick that up. You'll be constructing a timeline not only of the story, *but also of the backstory*, just as we did when we read about Jack and Jill. In some of your books, it might be helpful to do a personal timeline, of events in the character's life, as well as a historical timeline of the big historical events. Then you can see how those intersect. I'll be curious to see what kind of work you do with this."

Complex treatment of time will be especially challenging for your English language learners. Sentences will be especially complicated when the event that occurs later in the sentence actually occurs earlier in life, as in this example: I went to get lunch because I had been hungry all morning. You may want to lead small-group work with texts that are less complex than this one.

Note that links don't simply link the new teaching point to the children's independent work. Links also link the new work to prior learning. Readers are reminded to draw on all they have already learned, in addition to the new work of the day.

Actually, in books that are level U and V, it is not uncommon for the reader to still be learning the backstory as the reader approaches the ending of the actual story and the plotline. It is important to understand that at some levels, the backstory is leaked out, drip by drip, rather than provided in one spot early in the book.

Before sending children off to read, remind them to record information in their reading logs and to set a page goal with other club members.

"Club members, let me remind you of something that has been helping my club. Before you disperse to read, you'll want to be sure you agree upon your page goal, and remind each other of this goal even when you don't have a formal meeting. That way readers won't get ahead of our friends, which makes for uneven conversations, right? I almost got ahead of my club yesterday and had to remind myself to stop and read my other book. You'll also need to decide upon what work you'll be doing as readers. Will you continue to take notes by tacking important story elements onto a paper as you did yesterday? I'm hoping that among other things, you make a timeline of the story (and the backstory). Perhaps one person will do that for the whole club or perhaps you'll all do it? There may be other ways you'll capture your thinking. You know how to choose. Let's take just one minute (just sixty seconds) to settle upon the work you'll be doing. So take a moment to turn and talk, and then let's get the room quiet so readers can really focus."

You may find that children devote inordinate lengths of time determining the pages the club members plan to read before meeting again. If this consumes too much time, you will want to let club members know that it's inconceivable that a club would fritter away precious work time arguing over little details. Try insisting that the club be the one to invent a solution—almost any solution will do—because you are teaching toward self-reliance. If need be, however, you can share with them how other clubs have solved this problem, by scheduling the entire book on a calendar, for example, by marking it up with Post-its with dates on them, by figuring out chapter chunks that are close to fifty or sixty pages a day. If some members read more quickly, be sure they are also reading their independent books. Also—and this is important—be sure that club plans are not too modest to allow for the quantity of reading that readers need to be doing.

CONFERRING AND SMALL-GROUP WORK

Help Readers Engage in Skill Development Work

Teachers, your children will read as usual, and you'll confer into that reading as usual. We've designed the mid-workshop teaching point and the conferring and small group work differently to show that the first launches clubs today, and the latter discusses the teaching you do, not as children read, but as they work in those clubs.

MID-WORKSHOP TEACHING POINT

Readers Push to Deepen Our Conversations

I'd already gotten clubs started midway through the workshop, at this point, so this mid-workshop teaching point was actually a mid-club teaching point. "Readers, look up here, please. I want to share with you some work that the Freedom Fighters did today, because I think it will help all of us. The Freedom Fighters—Aly, Sam, Josh, Fallon, and Isaac—were talking about *The Gold Cadillac*, and they were trying to figure out this family's economic status. This story is all about a black family living during the Civil Rights Movement, and the big event is that the father goes out and buys a shiny new Cadillac (that's a very expensive car). The Freedom Fighters had read to the part where the dad brings the car home and he faces lots of different reactions. The children—the narrator and her older sister—are surprised, almost in disbelief that this new car really belongs to them. The neighbors are shocked and maybe a little envious. The dad is happy and proud, and the mother is displeased. She even refuses to ride in the car!

"The club wondered why the purchase of that car evoked such strong—and varied—reactions. What's interesting is that the members of the Freedom Fighters had different reactions, too. They didn't agree, but they kept talking about the details in their ideas, and going back to the story to show each other important parts. And that's how they came to some new thinking. It took a lot of back and forth in their conversation, and then the Freedom Fighters realized *collaboratively*, by putting all their ideas together, that this family doesn't have that much money. It makes sense that the mother is unhappy with this purchase; she's thinking practically, about money, and hoping to move her family to a better house in a safer neighborhood instead of having a new car. Meanwhile, the father is proud because a Cadillac makes him feel important—it is a big deal for a poor black family to have at that time. The

continued on next page

children, once they realize the car is really theirs, are thrilled. They love having something that fancy to show off to everyone, and they love riding around in it with their proud, happy daddy.

"What the Freedom Fighters eventually realized by talking so long, and with such detail, and listening to everyone's ideas, is that the purchase of a car had huge consequences to that particular family at that time. They also realized, as we discovered as a class when we examined how various characters reacted to the soldiers in Denmark in *Number the Stars*, that in historical fiction, you can learn a lot about the time period, and about the events of that period, by exploring how different characters—with their various perspectives—respond to one thing or another. That's important work, readers, and you'll want to consider that idea in your book clubs.

"But what's especially important about the Freedom Fighters' work is not just that they realized that we all can study how characters respond to events in the time period. It's that they were willing to work together to come to this realization. I've actually started a chart, because I think these habits will benefit my club as well." I gestured to the chart behind me and read the first bullet.

Growing Powerful Book Club Conversations

- *Be a good listener by leaning in, making eye contact, and letting the person speaking finish his or her thought. You can even jot notes as someone speaks, to honor his or her words.*

- *Be aware of any member who has gone unheard. Invite him or her in.*

continued from previous page

"I'm telling you this because I know, when I'm saying something in my club, that when my colleagues lean in and really look as if they want to know more, I am so glad to be in this club. The other day one of my colleagues even took notes when I said something, and that feels like such an honor.

"Just for the next couple of minutes, let's see what it looks and feels like when we really work on being active listeners who take note of each other's thoughts and honor fellow book club members, and are thoughtful friends to each other. Let's invite in our quiet friends as well as honor our active ones."

For the next three minutes or so, book clubs talked while I watched over, mostly not interfering. The goal was not to fix each club but to allow each club to experience their own best talking work, to build the "muscle memory" of what they can do independent of my help.

"Readers, we'll continue to build our chart of what it means to have powerful book club talk. For now, use everything you know—as you just did—to develop thoughtful habits that make others glad to be with us."

Conferring and Small-Group Work

Reading clubs offer you a perfect opportunity to provide differentiated instruction. You will have assessed your children and used those assessments plus the goals of your unit (and your year) to fashion some possible reading goals for your different clubs. When you meet with clubs to talk about those goals, you absolutely can consider showing them the evidence that you draw upon to derive goals. For example, if you've noticed that the children in one club tend to grow ideas about the main character only and rarely seem to pay attention to minor characters, you will want to show them what you noticed. You can show them that their books are changing, and so their reading work needs to change. They'll be glad for the challenge.

On the other hand, although you may say to children, "I've been studying the assessments, and I'm realizing you could profit from some work on. . . . Perhaps you want to invent some ways of working on that, and some artifacts that will show how you're getting better at it. . . ." The truth is that the assessments will never produce an agenda for all the readers in a club, so in the end, it's up to teachers to generate possible goals for a club. I find that it helps, in a conversation with the club members, if I suggest two or perhaps three possible goals and it also helps if I've got some energy around the sort of work that a club might do in pursuit of one goal or another.

In considering what the possible goals might be, you'll want to remember that although the unit of study is ostensibly on reading historical fiction,

the real goal is to help children tackle complex texts. That's a big goal, and there are many paths to that one goal. So whereas all of your children will, hopefully, be envisioning the world in which their stories are set, walking in the shoes of their characters, reading on the edges of their seats so they predict in ways that allow them to almost write the story that they haven't yet read, and learning to see layers of significance and meaning in their stories, individuals will engage in this work differently. Some will be flying through small, light texts, working on the tricky words that accompany historical settings and working to hold onto the problem-solution story line that spans their little stories. Others will lug gigantic tomes to and from school, immersed in the longest books they've ever read, and will work to keep the early parts of the book in mind as they read ravenously onward. You'll obviously steer clubs toward goals that take into account the challenges their texts tend to pose.

Rally Members of a Club Around a Shared Goal

It is important to me that volume and fluency work not fall by the wayside as we engage in the more sophisticated work this unit presents. Approaching the Civil War Club, I knew that they had read and talked about the picture book I'd suggested as a launching point for their club, *The Patchwork Path*, on the first day of clubs. They had rallied around Rosa's suggestion to continue the next day with another picture book, *Sweet Clara and the Freedom Quilt*, and then on to *Nettie's Trip South*. *Nettie's Trip South*, while also a picture book, contained more sophisticated language than the kids were used to, and I noticed that they were all still in the beginning section of the book, and for a book as short as this one, I felt they should be encouraged to progress a bit faster. I also knew that they'd be starting a chapter book soon, *Freedom's Wings*, that I suspected would pose some challenges for them and that they'd really need to be thinking about volume then. One reason for the slowdown with *Nettie's Trip South* was probably that they were encountering trickier words while simultaneously working to get a handle on the time period and the new perspective. The first books they'd read had been from the perspective of slaves, and this one was from the perspective of a Northerner observing slavery. I didn't want those things to make them founder though, stuck in the doldrums.

I decided to bring the challenge to them, saying, "So, I've noticed that you all seemed to have slowed way down in your reading since you started *Nettie's Trip South*. I wonder if it's taking a while to get used to the new things you're encountering in the book. I am thinking that you are working hard to pay attention to lots of new things—but guess what? Reading a lot each day is still really important. I wonder what you might be able to come up with that could help you read more and read smoothly."

After some discussion, Gabe came up with the idea to use a stopwatch periodically, timing their reading and keeping track of their times, as runners do. That was not really my first choice for a way for them to work on their pace and fluency, but I figured it wasn't going to do them any harm, and the idea was coming from them, which will in turn build energy, which will in turn help them read more. And the more they read, the more

smoothly they'd read as they became familiar with the time period, the style, and the vocabulary used.

In a similar way, I rallied the members of the Pioneers Club around the goal of bringing books to life. That goal is a broad one, but I had in mind some particular subgoals. One of those involved helping these readers read with increasing fluency. After I found a DVD of *Sarah, Plain and Tall* with Glenn Close, the Pioneers Club watched a short excerpt, paying close attention to how the actors said the book's words, and then they tried to bring that same level of drama and engagement into their own voices as they read aloud. This club and the Civil War Club did dramatic readings of parts of their books. It was also important to me to rally these kids around the goal of seriously ramping up their volume of reading. I said to the members of that club, "Can I tell you about some really important research that grown-ups have been doing about young readers, because I think it applies to you. Some researchers have been suggesting that kids need to be actually reading—eyes-on-print reading—something like ninety minutes a day, which means something like seventy pages a day. That can include reading in social studies and science and all—and I know you do some of that—but that research finding really means that you all need to push yourselves to read tons more. Not just a little more—but a whole lot more."

Of course, it was key to learn suggestions the club members had for how they could reach toward this goal. Their suggestions often aren't perfect ones, but few things matter more than that people have a sense of agency, of "I can gather all my resources to rise to this challenge." Sometimes a club may decide to meet a bit less often than other clubs to reserve more class time for reading, or they may agree that if their club conversation is lagging, they will sometimes shift back to more reading. The Pioneers Club decided that maintaining and researching their reading logs should become a club ritual. I pointed out that when they looked at their logs, they needed to look not only for whether club members were doing the minimum of reading, but also for times people were getting lost in books. The club members agreed that this month, they would try to read a whole tower of books, reading one right after the next, at a good clip. They'd already finished reading a picture book—*Dandelions*, by Eve Bunting—and agreed that then they would tackle the first three books of the *Sarah, Plain and Tall* series. They also had plans to potentially read another chapter book, *The Cabin Faced West*. They even made a reading schedule for the next two weeks.

The Intersection Between a Unit of Study and a Reading Club's Own Goals

The fact that each club adopts a goal that spans the entire unit doesn't mean the clubs don't participate in work that is supported by whole-class instruction—far from it! But, for example, when the Civil War Club worked to construct a personal timeline for one of their characters, because this club had adopted fluency as one of their goals, members of that club didn't just *talk about* the scenes that should be on that timeline (wrestling with which scenes did and which did not merit stars for being turning points). They also reread those scenes repeatedly, each time trying on different interpretations.

Meanwhile, the Freedom Fighters, the club that tackled the goal of thinking deeply about characters, didn't just put historical events on the timeline. They also wrestled with how different characters responded differently to each of those events. Our conferences and our work with clubs, then, will come from a wonderful intersection of class work, the club's own agenda, individual reader's trajectories, and the specifics of that day.

A Conference that Is Typical of Many You'll Lead Early in the Unit

When I pulled my chair alongside the Freedom Fighters Club, I noted they had completed the picture book, *Freedom Summer* and were well into Mildred Taylor's *The Gold Cadillac*. As always, I signaled for the club members to ignore me and continue talking.

Isaac read a Post-it aloud. *[Fig. IV-2]*

Fallon had been listening keenly enough to hear the contradiction in Isaac's Post-it (which impressed me) and called Isaac on it. "You just said they're middle class (cause they have the car and all), but *then* you said they're so poor. They can't be *both* in the middle *and* poor."

Isaac was unfazed, suggesting that his whole point had been that different people thought differently about this. Sam added his two cents. "I think they're middle class, 'cause they have the money to buy a fancy new Cadillac. *But*, it seems like they live in a poor neighborhood, so maybe they're saving to buy a house." Sam didn't refer to his Post-it, but it had clearly prompted his comment. *[Fig. IV-3]* Aly disagreed, pointing out that the children's relatives had been flabbergasted by the car.

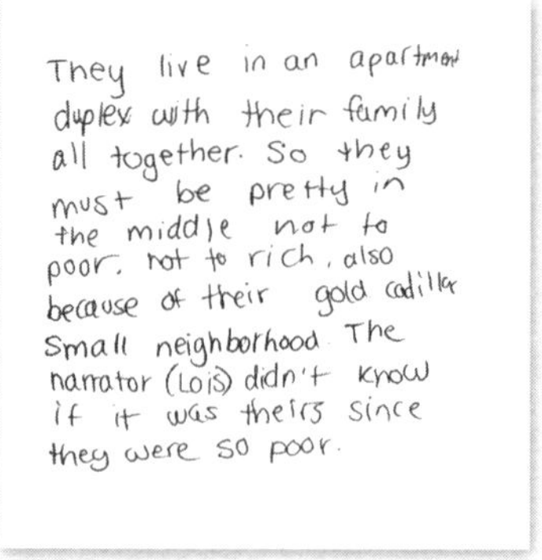

Figure IV-2

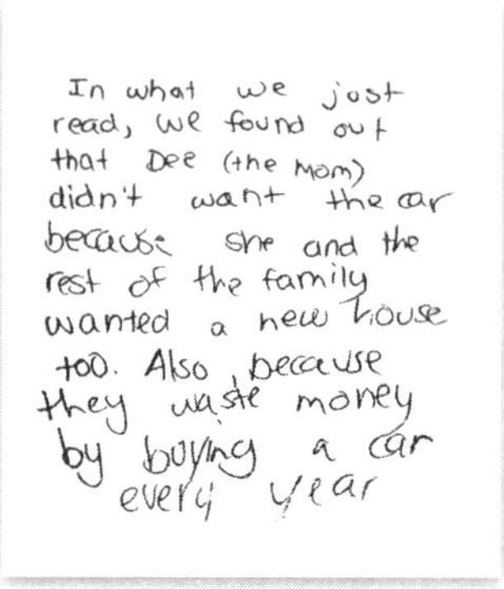

Figure IV-3

At this point, I jumped in. "I love that you are trying to come to consensus about the basic facts of this story. And I love that you are actually talking back and forth about an idea, not just jumping from one idea to another one. But I want to point out that the confusion you are feeling right now is totally a part of reading. It will happen often when you read, that you are a bit unclear about something essential to the story. Are these people poor—or middle class? I am pretty sure that instead of just pulling guesses out of the sky, you can figure out a really smart way to clear up this kind of confusion when it happens." I was quite sure I didn't need to be the one to name that this was a good time for the readers to return to the text. How frequently that happens—that book clubs get going, talking up a storm, and no one has the book open!

Soon the children had turned back to the text, but their search didn't yield a definitive answer. "Don't expect the author to come right out and spell things out for you," I said in a voiceover, just before the chorus began of, "She doesn't say." "The author will give you hints, that's all, and expect that you are able to figure it out."

Aly wondered if the fact that the mother didn't like the car could be a hint. "On page 13, it says, 'There was no smile on her face.' And later, the dad says, 'Now stop frowning, honey, and let's take ourselves for a ride in our brand-new Cadillac!' So that shows the mom didn't like the car, and that's a hint." The kids asked how that connected in any way. Hadn't Aly just switched to a whole new topic? Aly said that, no, what she was trying to say was that maybe the mother didn't like the car because she didn't want to waste money on a car 'cause they weren't rich, and she wanted to pay the rent. The children nodded, agreeing this was a possibility but made no move to research this further in the text—even though a minute earlier, when they'd encountered a different question, I'd nudged them to do just that.

So I intervened. "Let me see. Am I right that you have reached a point in the discussion where you are not sure, yes or no, whether the mother resists the car because she is worrying whether the family can afford it? You're not sure whether the book agrees with that idea or not? I'm wondering how you could find that out. Hmm, . . ."

The children belatedly got the hint and began looking in the text for evidence that the father was an overly big spender in the family. In the process, Aly stumbled on the line that the car was "like no car we had ever owned before" and that it "looked like a car for rich folks."

"So they're not rich!" Josh said enthusiastically.

"Wow," I said. "Do you see how far you've come in this one conversation just by trying to come to enough of a consensus that you could tack up the basic facts about who this book is about, where they live, and so forth? You have even decided the family's income level. More than this,

you learned to do some important things. You've disagreed with each other—and lots of clubs never do that, so congratulations for listening closely enough to hear contradictions in what someone says or to hear logic you don't buy. And when you came to questions, over and over you thought to yourselves, 'Let's look again at the text and see exactly what it does say.'"

I asked the children what they would think about next. They figured they'd read and see what else came to mind. "You could do that," I said. "But it is really helpful to do what readers refer to as 'following a line of questioning.' So you figured out that the family is really poor, but even so, for some reason the father went and bought this super-expensive car. What might be the logical next question to ask?"

The children agreed that it was probably important for them to try to understand why the father wanted that car, why it was so important to him that he got it when the family might need that money for rent. They were off and running, and I moved to another club. Later, however, I peeked at their Post-its and saw their thinking had continued to evolve. [Figs. IV-4 and IV-5]

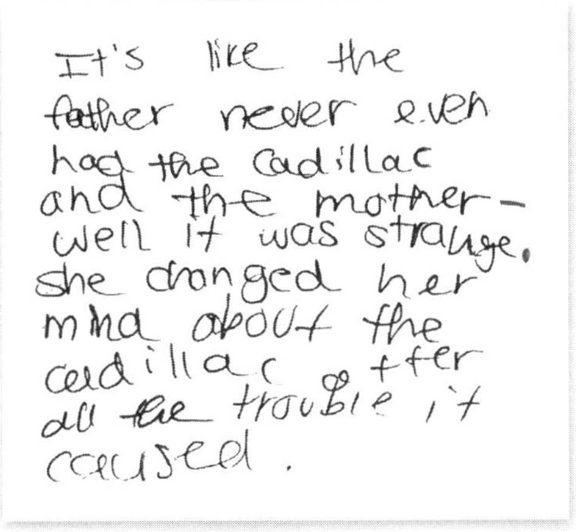

It's like the father never even had the Cadillac and the mother—well it was strange. she changed her mind about the cadillac after all the trouble it ccaused.

Figure IV-4

What does the Gold Cadalac 3/9 represent?
· The fight between mom and dad!??
· The fact that mother won't use the Cadalac
· She is afraid because WHITES HATE blacks having nicer things than them, that car is nice for a white man. They don't, won't, take that.
· Blacks don't get treated well in the first place.

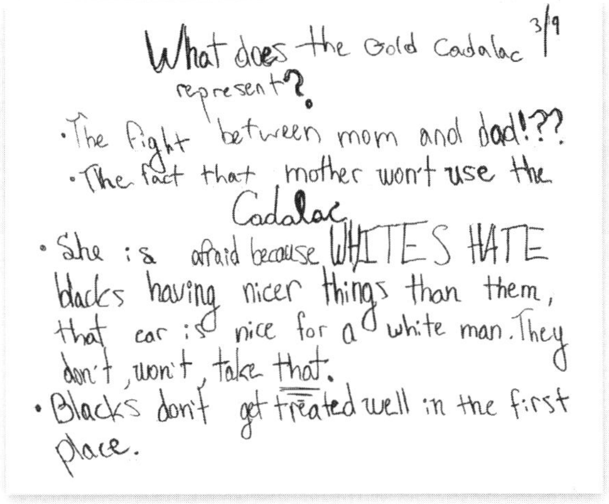

Figure IV-5

TEACHING SHARE

Readers Use Writing and Graphic Organizers as Tools for Thought

Challenge your students to think and talk about their intentions when making timelines and other graphic organizers.

After readers talked in their clubs for about five minutes, I intervened to ask for the whole class's undivided attention. After making sure all eyes were on me, I said, "Readers, I know you are dying to keep talking, but I need to ask you a question. I'm noticing that all of your clubs have made timelines of the events in your books, and I need to ask you—why have you done that? I don't get it."

The kids looked at me, flabbergasted, one kid linking eyes with the next as if to say, "Is she losing it?"

One brave soul started to sputter out, "*You* told us to make timelines." I held up my hand. I was going to have none of that. This, of course, riled them all up even more. Several kids were just about to combine their efforts to convince me that honest, I truly *had* told them to do this, when I started to speak. "I know full well you are all saying that you made timelines because I told you to do so, and I am not arguing that I told you to do so. But that doesn't take away the fact that you need to take this job on, and any job that anyone gives you, as your own personal project. Remember, one person digging a hole will be digging because he has been told to do so—and another will be digging for treasure. You have a choice in life. You can make a timeline because I told you to do so, or you can make a timeline because this is a powerful way to push your thinking.

"If I went so far as to suggest someone from each club might record a timeline and to ask that your clubs talk first about those timelines, you can be sure I wasn't suggesting you waste your time on a meaningless ho-hum exercise. Did you ever stop to think, 'Why are we doing this?'

"Try thinking about that right now. Think, 'Once I've recorded the sequence of important events in a story and I'm holding that sequence in my hand, what sort of further thinking can I now do?'

COACHING TIPS

You'll want to remember that in the link at the end of today's minilesson, I sent children out to read, asking them to make timelines of the sequence of events in their stories as they read. The share was designed with full awareness that I'd given those instructions. If you don't channel kids to make timelines, this share won't work, which would be fine. Invent another!

One of the things we know about teaching is that repetition counts. If you and I have a concept that we believe really matters, we can't just mention it one day, in passing, and assume that all our students have taken in what we said. You may at first glance think that this is a minilesson about timelines, but of course it is not. The minilesson is saying to kids, "You are the author of your own reading life. It will always be—for each of us—My Life, by me. And as part of that, you have big decisions to make. Will you dig a hole as if you are a hired manual laborer, or will you dig as if for gold? Will you read and live as if you are a curmudgeon or as if the text is gold? There have probably been a dozen times throughout the past few units of study when you have made the same point, but it bears being made yet again and again. The challenge is to find new ways to say the same ol' thing. The challenge is to actually make contact, to actually engage kids in the biggest project of them all—that of constructing themselves.

"Do you suppose that everyone agrees that the timeline one person made of a book is a perfect timeline of that book? Might some people think the timeline is missing really important moments—or that the spaces between the moments are accurate? Is there other thinking you could do off your timelines?" I asked and was quiet. "Might you each star the moment you regard as an especially important one and then talk between each other's ideas?"

Remind your students that strong clubs invest their graphic organizers and other tools with their clubs' own intentions. Ask your students to set themselves up for the next couple of days' reading work.

"Right now, talk among your club about whether you used the timeline you made as a tool for thought, or did you just make it because you were told to do so? You could ask yourselves the same thing about notes you have made about characters. Then return to your club conversations, but this time remember that your club is just that—*your* club. Make everything you do work for you.

This time as the clubs worked together, I helped them make sure their timelines and other notes supported deep thinking. One club timelined how the mood of the setting changed, for example.

When it came time to end the workshop, I said, "Clubs, time to set your goalpost for tonight's reading and, actually, for the reading you will do in school tomorrow and at home tomorrow because we're going to spend more time reading tomorrow and not get into clubs until the day after. Remember that in general, you should be able to read at least twenty pages in school and again, twenty to thirty more pages at home, and probably a lot more than that, in a day. So you may aim to be at least eighty pages farther in your book before your club meets again, unless there are reasons to be reading more slowly."

Graphic organizers are hot items in the field of education today, and some of you will be pleased to see them surfacing in this series. I hope you notice that children are making their own drawings—their own timelines in this instance and their own Venn diagrams in another instance. I think that if we really want learners to understand that part of learning is sorting ideas into structures (which I do believe is important), then we need to let the learners themselves make the structures, and the more informal and temporary they are, the better. In the end, very few of us make physical timelines or Venn diagrams as we read! Instead, we create mental models, and those mental models may take the shape of timelines, Venn diagrams, outlines, or grids. Hopefully, our young people grow up building their own thought structures, their own mental models.

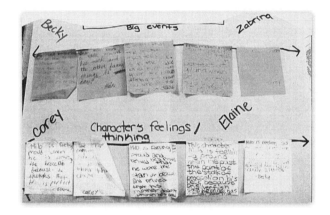

Think of charts like these as temporary tools of thought, not as art projects or material for display.

Unfolding Characters While Unfolding History

e've delved into how time shifts in the stories we encounter, showing our readers how the story line will often be interrupted with passages that give a backstory, with descriptions of or references to earlier events that give us a deeper understanding of the background. These are complicated time shifts, and as books begin to embed them, simple timelines become a valuable tool for keeping track of and remembering events.

Another way that timelines can be useful is to track the emergence of parallel and converging histories. In historical fiction, there is often a historical drama, against which emerges a personal drama. It's often helpful for readers to sketch a quick timeline of historical events and next to that timeline a timeline of the personal events in the character's life. When you do this, you'll often gain insight into the relationship between these timelines. Are the big events in a character's life influenced by historical events? Is there a sense of story lines that run parallel or that converge?

For your readers, you'll probably want to start by teaching them to keep track of both the historical narrative and the personal narrative of the main character. Because readers will also be reading more than one text in their historical period, you have an opportunity to show them that as they read a second related text, they can return to their historical timeline, filling it in. They'll learn to fill in their historical timelines with more detail and predict how certain events in their second or

GETTING READY

- Prior to teaching today's minilesson—preferably just prior to it—you will need to have finished reading Chapter 2 of *Number the Stars* aloud to children so that during today's session you can ask children to sketch a timeline of Annemarie's life and the sequence of historical events that unfold around that chapter.

- You'll need chart paper or a white board on hand to make two timelines during this day's minilesson.

- During the teaching portion of today's minilesson, you will need to be prepared to show the personal timeline of your life, your plotline, and show how it is intertwined with historical events of the time in which you have lived.

- Then you and your students will work together to create a timeline of events unfolding in the read-aloud—both a timeline of the protagonist's life and one of the historical events of the time.

- Provide each club with a passage from their book that contains significant details about historical events that they can reread to practice today's work. This will take some time for browsing.

- During the mid-workshop teaching point, which should come once kids have already begun their work in clubs for the day, you will introduce the "Making Our Way Through Historical Fiction" chart.

third stories may unfold, based on what they have learned about the time period. All of these timelines are first done concretely, with pencils, and eventually become mental or virtual tools that readers construct during reading.

It's safe to assume that in the books your students are reading, the characters are strongly influenced by the unfolding of historical events. Sometimes the historical events make themselves felt as a force right away, as in

> *Simple timelines become one of our most useful tools for keeping track of and remembering events while reading.*

Number the Stars and *Rose Blanche*. Other times, the historical pressures emerge gradually, seeping into the characters' and the reader's consciousness, as with *The Watsons Go to Birmingham*. Either way, the historical events exert tremendous pressure on the characters and the setting. Ishmael Beah's greatest worry might have been hip-hop contests, until he got caught in a war and taken up as a child soldier, as he depicts in *A Long Way Gone*. And the Watsons' trip to Birmingham wouldn't have merited the same effect on Kenny if it hadn't occurred at a time when a southern church was attacked. In most historical fiction, as in most complex novels, the setting does far more than provide a passive backdrop. You'll recall that earlier I described the setting in historical fiction as a convergence of time and place. We are now asking children to understand that this mix of time and place that combines to form a story's setting is not just the backdrop, not just a parallel timeline, but

instead, this context actually affects (and even almost determines) the plot.

Comprehending the influence of historical events is harder for young readers than for us. First of all, they simply don't know as much about history. References that are familiar to us are often experienced by them as mysterious clues. Historical trajectories that we have known for years, through many stories, unroll for the first time for them in the stories they are reading. The books may also contain a complex treatment of time, where the historical backstory reveals itself even as character's backstory reveals itself. Even strong readers may find themselves gaping silently when you ask, "How does the time period, the historical events, affect this character's choices?"

It is helpful to think of the mental models that help us, as adult readers, through the complexity of multiple plotlines and treatments of time. To do this, we take the two tangled threads of a character's *personal* life and of the *historical* events that occur alongside that personal life, and we separate those threads for just a moment so we can examine how they work—alone first, and then again, interwoven. We aim for these timelines to be visual representations of the thinking that will enable our young readers to negotiate the complex treatments of time and plot in their own novels. Of course, once we do this work visually, we provide children with a tool that will be used in increasingly complex ways over time. Even if they don't actually sit and draw timelines of the historical fiction that they read now and later in life, we hope that timelines will be charted on their mental terrain as they progress through books, giving them a place to mark and keep track of forthcoming detail as they read.

In using separate timelines to discuss the plot of historical fiction, we are developing our own unique discourse, our classroom's special vocabulary and language for tackling historical fiction, and complex texts, in a specific way. Club discussions will reflect these ways of thinking, but ultimately, like all scaffolding, these will be left behind. Don't worry that this tool is too simple. Pick up *War and Peace*. You'll find yourself sketching timelines in your mind!

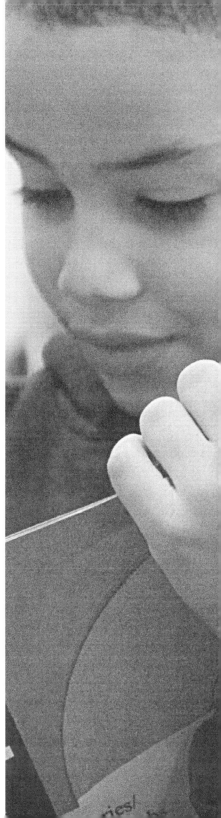

MINILESSON

Unfolding Characters While Unfolding History

CONNECTION

Tell children about how people you know responded to a big event in history, illustrating the way historical events initiate many cause-and-effect sequences.

"Readers, I recently finished a book about a woman from Michigan who used to be a housewife and hairdresser in a small American town. Following September 11th, she joined a humanitarian agency that took her to Kabul, Afghanistan, where she thought she'd help out as a nurse's assistant. Instead, she became the head of a beauty institute that helped train Afghan women to run beauty parlors. The Taliban had shut down all beauty parlors in that country until this American woman helped reopen a few. 'In a country that has little social recreation for women,' she wanted to know, 'where else will women relax and gossip, if not at the hairdressers?'

"This book got me thinking about all the people I know and people I've read about whose lives have changed forever because of September 11th. There's this hairdresser from a small American town who became a controversial figure in Afghanistan. A man I know became a grief counselor after meeting one of the affected families. Spouses of the men and women who lost their lives that day became advocates for peace. When this one big thing happened, so many New Yorkers and, indeed, so many people around the world, found the plotline of their own lives changed."

If we follow strict definitions of formal history, perhaps not enough time has elapsed since September 11th for it to be considered a "historical" occurrence. It is on purpose that in this particular connection, I draw on a monumental event that is recent and familiar enough to have left its indelible mark on students' subconsciousness. Mention of the World Trade Center tragedy does, after all, recall a sense of a Big Thing That Affects Us All. Children—indeed many adults—tend to view history as something that has no relevance outside of textbooks. I'm hoping in this familiar example to reach for the sense of history being full of big things that affect us all.

Extrapolate a larger message. History is comprised of many Big Things, each altering the course of people's lives, creating small personal stories.

"Readers, history is made up of big things that happen to a society, to a country, to the world. And these big things affect the lives of all the people living at that time in some way. As readers of historical fiction, we become even more aware that the wars and movements and discoveries and revolutions that we read about in history textbooks actually *happened* in the lives of ordinary people like you and me. There's the official history of the big things that happened (I made a big sweeping gesture), and then

In the Common Core Standards, it is especially important for students to be able to think across big ideas, seeing relationships between one set of ideas and another. You are supporting this intellectual work within this unit.

there are the small personal stories of the people who had to cope through them (I formed waves with my hands to show these functioned as little ripples, wafting out from the events).

State your teaching point. Specifically tell children that readers of historical fiction consider both the big historical timeline of things as well as the smaller individual timelines of characters' lives that occur alongside these.

"What I want to teach you today is that in historical fiction, there are many timelines. There is the main character's timeline—a timeline that is a personal narrative or plot-line—and there is a historical timeline of the big historical events. And the two are entwined. This is also true in life itself. The events in the main character's life—in your life and mine—occur alongside, and are affected by, an unfolding timeline of world events. To understand a character, a person, we have to get to know not only the person's personal timeline but also the historical timeline that winds in and out of the personal timeline.

TEACHING

Retell your personal timeline, or plotline, and a parallel historical timeline to provide a real-life example of how an individual's choices (yours) are affected by historical context.

"I could make a personal timeline of my life. It might start like this:

- 1951: Born in Boston, Massachusetts

- 1960: Moved to a farm in western New York

- 1961: Started middle school. Don Graves was my minister.

- 1961–1965: Painful Middle School. Began tutoring reading

- 1965–1969: High School (tutoring)

"But I could also make a timeline, beside my personal timeline, of some of the events in history that were happening as I grew up. The start of that timeline might look like this:

Children have a hard time thinking about history with any sense of relativity. Hundreds of years can, for them, get lumped together into "the olden days." Later in the unit, you'll see that the children construct a class timeline. For example, in this class, the timeline contains World War I, and near that place on the timeline, the children will hang the book jacket to Letters from Rifka, *which is an immigration story about a Jewish family that is seeking refuge in America, set in 1919. The anti-Semitism in that story takes on greater significance because this story occurs just twenty years before* Number the Stars, *which of course tells of Nazi soldiers on every corner in Denmark and of the Jewish families being rounded up and deported. Alongside World War II on the timeline (1942) there will be a photo of the book cover for* Number the Stars. *Such a timeline can help children begin to think of their stories in relation to each other.*

You will want to have prepared your version of a bulleted list and of the chart below for your children to see as you talk. Or, if you'd rather not use your own timeline, you could easily substitute the timeline of someone you know, saying "This is the timeline of my friend's life."

Personal

- 1951: Born in Boston, Massachusetts

- 1960: Moved to a farm in western New York. My parents built a bomb shelter in basement.

- 1961: Teased in middle school. Don Graves was my minister.

  Began tutoring reading in urban Lackawanna

- 1965–1969: High School (tutoring)

Historical

- 1951: Color TV introduced in U.S.
  Sputnik
  Berlin Wall erected.

- 1960: Beatles formed

- 1961: JFK inaugurated. Peace Corps. Camelot.

- 1963: March on Washington
  JFK assassinated.
  Tension between U.S. and USSR

- 1964: Gulf of Tonkin—Vietnam War

- 1968: Dr. Martin Luther King, Jr., assassinated
  My Lai Massacre

- 1969: Neil Armstrong walks on the moon.

"For someone to understand the story of my life, it helps for that person to know not only the sequence of my personal timeline, or plotline, but for that person to also know the unfolding events in the world (I pointed to the right side of the timeline) that influenced my personal timeline. I'm going to tell you my life story. Listen to how my life has been shaped by the historical events of the times. Every time I mention something in the world that affected my unfolding life, would you point this way (I tipped my thumbs up toward the right-hand column, where I'd listed the historical events of the times). When I mention something new in my personal timeline, point toward that timeline (I tipped my thumbs up signal to the left).

"During my middle school years there was a lot of unrest in the world." I waited to see if the kids signaled, and then tipped my thumb to the right to remind them. "East Germany erected the Berlin Wall, our country's relations with the former USSR (now Russia) were strained, the USSR detonated a huge fifty-megaton hydrogen bomb to form the world's largest man-made explosion. The world felt scary. My parents built a cement bomb shelter in our basement that they stocked up with canned goods (I

You will find that this exercise is riveting for your students, particularly if you use your own timeline. It can be interesting as well to have students think about how they themselves are situated in history and how their own timelines are affected by what's happening in the world!

tipped my thumb to the left) just in case. In school we had practice air raids during which we'd line up against the wall with our arms up over our heads (left). And for me, the world was also scary because like Rob, I was preyed upon by kids with more power (left).

"The United States became involved in a war in Vietnam. There were peace protests and marches on Washington. Civil rights activists like Dr. Martin Luther King, Jr., fought for freedom, using the churches, the schools, and the courts to press their movement forward (right). At the same time, an exciting speaker, Don Graves, became the head of the youth ministry at our church. Don would later lead the writing process movement and bring me along in it. At that time, I felt safe and important in the youth projects he led at the church, especially when I was tutoring reading near the steel plant (left). In the world, too, there seemed to be more hope. John F. Kennedy, who'd become president in 1961, established the Peace Corps and talked about service: 'Ask not what your country can do for you; ask what you can do for your country' (right). School segregation (that means black and white children attending different schools) was coming to what people thought would be an end in the South. People were working together to try to create a more peaceful world. The Beatles sang songs of peace and love.

"You can stop making the signals because you're going to want to just listen to what happened to me and to the world next.

"And then came November 22, 1963. The day JFK was shot. I'd just upset my teacher in homemaking class by sewing a seam on a skirt backward. I remember that everyone was astir as I made my way from the outbuilding where the class was held to our main building. As soon as I entered the main school, I saw teachers huddled in the hallway, weeping. 'What happened?' I asked. 'He's dead.' They all said.

"JFK was a bit like President Obama is to many people today. Over the days after Kennedy's death, I remember thinking about his famous words, 'Ask not what your country can do for you; ask what you can do for your country.' I began to mentor myself to people who wanted to improve conditions for all. I tried not to despair over the randomness of Kennedy's assassination, or the brutality of Dr. Martin Luther King's. I didn't know it when I was young, but all of the events of that time shaped who I became and my decision to be a teacher."

Constructing the two timelines and the coherent story of them was actually not easy to do because of course there are a million historical events that occurred, and only some felt consequential to the very brief personal timeline. It would have been easier to proceed dot by dot, telling what was going on in the world and then telling what I recall of my relationship to each of those dots, those events. But it seemed important to create a intertwined personal plotline and historical timeline showing how the moments on both timelines linked together in a somewhat cause-and-effect, integrated way. You'll find this work is fascinating if you try it, shedding very intriguing light on your own life. I found it astonishing to realize that, indeed, these historical events probably did play a role in my life story—something that had never occurred to me until I did this work. Try it.

Those of us who lived through JFK's assassination, the Vietnam War, Kent State, and Birmingham have pretty explicit consciousness of how history has affected us. Younger colleagues, give this a try. You might be surprised to see how the falling of the Berlin Wall, the destruction of the World Trade Centers, the launching of the Iraq war, the election of Obama have affected your values, beliefs, actions, and choices. Your teaching will be more powerful if you draw on your own life story. [Figs. V-1 and V-2]

Suggest that a historical timeline forms the backdrop to any historical fiction novel, including the read-aloud. Show the children that you have started to make two time-lines for the read-aloud—a historical one and a timeline of the main character's life.

"There is a historical timeline that forms the backdrop to *Number the Stars*, too. Usually, when I read a historical fiction story, I keep track of these timelines mentally until I get confused, and then I begin jotting. Let me show you how I started two time-lines, one for historical events and the other for the characters, for Chapter 1 of *Number the Stars*:

Historical timeline

- 3 yrs. ago, German soldiers occupy Copenhagen.
- Some Danish people work as the Resistance to bring harm to the Nazis however they can.

Personal timeline

- Annemarie and Ellen run into German soldiers on the corner. Kirsti does too but is unconcerned.
- Ellen's mother stops having coffee with Annemarie's mother and retreats, worried, to her apartment when she hears of the girls' encounter.

"Notice that the main character's timeline, the personal narrative, starts with the first event in the book: Annemarie and Ellen run into the German soldiers. The historical timeline begins three years earlier, when the Germans first began occupying Copenhagen (remember Annemarie saying that in the three years since the soldiers arrived, they still hadn't learned to speak Danish).

"As you can see, I filled in the events as I learned about them in Chapter 1."

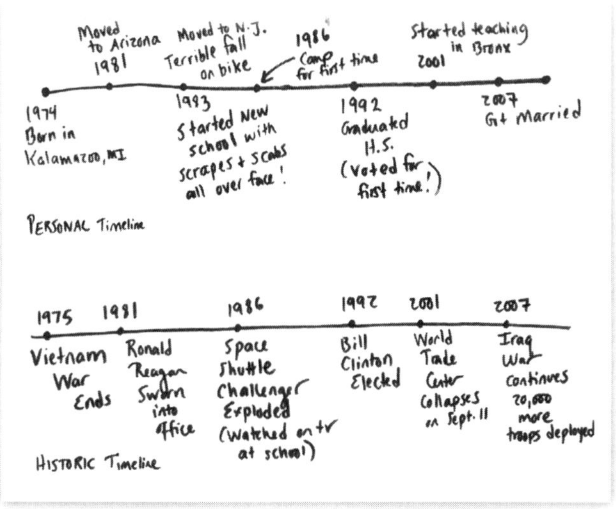

Figure V-1

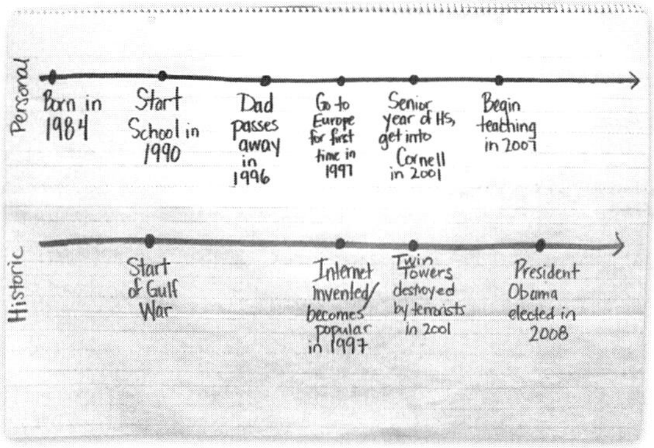

Figure V-2

For me, it makes sense to draw two timelines to signify that the two sets of events truly are unfolding in a "parallel" manner. Of course, you might choose another way to visually represent the intersection of the personal and the historical timelines. You could use two different color Post-its, one color for events on the character's personal timeline and another for events on the historical timeline, all on a single timeline if that feels like the most clear representation to you. You'll have to experiment with what works best in your particular classroom, with your particular kids.

ACTIVE INVOLVEMENT

Invite children, who will be sitting with their club mates in the meeting area, to help each other record information from the most recent chapter, Chapter 2, on a co-constructed timeline of Annemarie's life and a parallel historical timeline.

"In the second chapter, the author fills in more of the backstory. Remember, it starts with Kirsti and Annemarie in bed, and the little sister asking the big sister for a make-believe story about a king? Nothing else really happens in the chapter. Annemarie is still in bed with her sister at the end of the chapter, but her sister has fallen asleep. But in the pages of the chapter, Annemarie remembers the story of another king, and some other things, too, things that actually happened earlier in Annemarie's life. Let's try to recall what the chapter said about events that go earlier on Annemarie's plotline and on this historical timeline of the world. I'll give you a few minutes to talk in clubs while sitting right here in the meeting area. As you discuss, you can jot down the events that you're remembering on either the main plotline timeline or the historical timeline in your reading notebook. This will give you a feel for how these timelines help you to synthesize the personal and historical narratives."

Children added another event to the personal timelines: Some add that Annemarie tells Kirsti a story of a pretend king. Others add that Annemarie recalls seeing Denmark's real king and learning that every Danish citizen is his bodyguard. A different version of the latter event can actually go on the personal timeline. On Annemarie's timeline, her father tells her the story of King Christian. On the historical one, King Christian defies the German soldiers and rides through Copenhagen. [Figs. V-3 and V-4]

To the same timeline, they added a bit of backstory: Annemarie's sister, Lise, had been about to marry Peter when she died in an accident at the age of eighteen. I jotted this in front of the events from the first chapter (Annemarie and Ellen running into the soldier) because these events had already happened.

To the historical timeline, children added that the Nazis fought fiercely in Norway. Denmark instead agreed to neutrality because of their small size. Sweden was still a free country.

As you circulate, help children remember what happened in the read-aloud. You may distribute a few copies of the book for children to scan. Support readers as they determine importance so they can decide which events merit going on the timeline. Some readers also might need help jotting down the events in chronological order, rather than in the order in which they learn about them in the book.

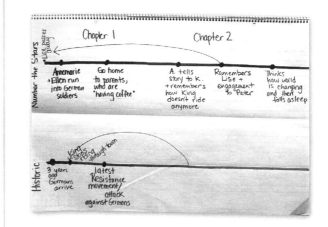

Figure V-3
You will add onto the timeline as you read aloud.

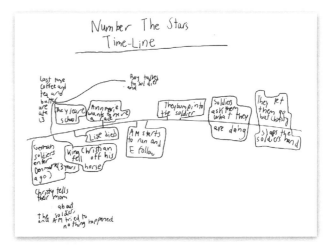

Figure V-4

Emphasize that readers think between the evolving historical context and the narrative plotline of the main character, noting how historical events affect characters' values, choices, and actions and noting that different characters have different perspectives on the same event.

"Readers I want to stress that when we read historical fiction and, really, any complicated stories, we construct several timelines—at least one of the main character and one of important historical events. Here is the thing: We also *think between those timelines*. To understand characters' actions, readers need to keep in mind that those actions are sometimes caused not by events on the *personal* plotline but by events on the *historical* timeline. In some of your books, you may find it helpful to keep personal plotlines for more than one character, as well.

LINK

Channel children to add these kinds of timelines to their repertoire as readers. You may also show them how to use a historical timeline within the book they are currently reading and across more than one book in a historical era to synthesize events in their stories.

"Readers, I think this tool is a really useful one, and I encourage you to take a few moments in the company of your club, to see how charting personal and historical timelines for the book your club is reading may give you fresh insights. Here's another suggestion as well that you may find helpful. You are reading several texts in a historical era. When you are engaged in a deep study that way, you often find that you can begin a historical timeline in one book and keep adding to it and using it as you move to the next story, so that you come to the second and third story with deeper understanding of the significance of historical events. You'll find you understand each of the books—and characters and moments in history—in deeper ways. *[Fig. V-5]*

This minilesson mainly attempts to teach readers to keep several timelines unfurling as they read—a skill that is crucial when reading historical fiction and important when reading any complex fiction. In books that are level R and beyond, readers are expected to learn vicariously as they read, to come to know unfamiliar places and themes by reading about them. That is, readers are expected to snowball information about the place and the time in which the story is set and about any issue or topic that is dominant in the story. The emphasis on creating two simultaneous timelines is an important one.

The upcoming minilesson will take a step further and also attempt to teach readers that it is important to notice the different ways in which characters react to any one event. This is really the start to teaching perspective, because the different reactions to the one event are driven by different perspectives, different points of view. This is a huge topic and one that will resurface later in the unit.

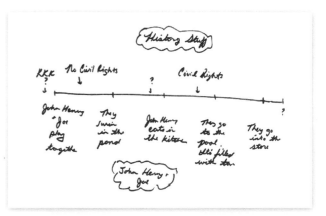

Figure V-5
The Freedom Fighters Club made a timeline of *Freedom Summer.*

"I invite you, right now, sitting here, to try this work in your books. Across your fingers or with quick jotting, piece together the timeline of historical events that is unrolling in the backdrop of *your* story. I'm going to give you just a minute to do this quickly and to talk with someone else who knows your book.

"Readers, sometimes your book does not come right out and explicitly tell you even a single historical event. It'll reveal the era when the story took place—you can see that if you look—but sometimes you won't find the historical events that were going on around then without asking someone or reading something outside your book. That's true in the Pioneers Club's *Sarah, Plain and Tall*. When that happens, you can still make and think about personal timelines, and eventually, when you also read nonfiction material available about the same time period, you'll learn about the historical timeline, and this will deepen your understanding of your main character's experiences.

Long before the children finished their conversations, I interrupted. "It is time to get started on your reading. As you read, remember to pay attention to the different timelines unfolding in your stories—the characters' personal timelines and the historical timeline. You know to decide on your goalpost page and get started wisely. Nice work."

Your students will probably want to talk about this for longer than the time you have to give them right now, but treat this just as a sort of "priming the pump" of their thinking to get them ready to do more of this work as they read and as they talk later.

A number of children were looking back and forth between the members of their club, silent. What did I mean about the historical timeline in their books? Sure there were historical facts in Number the Stars, *but those weren't so evident in* Sarah, Plain and Tall, *or in* Autumn Street. *They're right and for now, the easiest plan would be for them to draw upon a different text.*

CONFERRING AND SMALL-GROUP WORK

Help Readers Turn Passing Comments into Sustainable Inquiries

If your clubs will be working together for a little over ten minutes at the end of the reading workshop, aim to work with two clubs within that time. Of course, during the reading workshop itself, you'll also confer. Some of your conferring will support kids' actual reading. If you are unclear of ways to confer into the reading itself, reread some of the conferring sections from the final sessions of the character unit, especially. For now, my discussion of conferring and small-group work will focus more on the teaching you'll do to support the small-group structure of clubs.

Because club members will be sitting near each other as they read, from time to time you'll suggest a club meet together while other children are reading, just so you have the chance to help yet another club. Early in the unit, it is quite urgent for you to work with many clubs and to help each of those clubs feel as if they are working together with energy on work that matters.

> ## MID-WORKSHOP TEACHING POINT (TO LAUNCH CLUBS)
>
> ### Readers Rehearse for Club Meetings
>
> "Readers, all eyes up here. I'm wondering if any of you have been in a play or a concert? Did you all rehearse for the play? The concert?" The kids said yes, absolutely, of course. "I'm asking because club meetings, like plays and concerts, go better if readers take a few minutes before the club meets to rehearse, reading over our notes, thinking over our reading, and planning for what we'll bring to the club meeting. Right now, think, 'How will I rehearse for my club? How will I make sure I am bringing something worthy?'" I was quiet, scanning the room. When I saw a couple of readers who seemed unsure of what to do, I gestured toward an anchor chart that showed the work readers do at the beginning of historical fiction books. "If you need some suggestions, you could look at the record of the reading work we've been pursuing and think, 'What of that work makes the most sense for me right now?' I've added a few items to our chart to reflect additional work we've been doing recently.
>
> *continued on next page*

Conferring with the Freedom Fighters: A Graphic Organizer Can Focus the Energies of a Club

When I drew my chair alongside the Freedom Fighters Club, my first goal was to check to see whether they would be able to get involved with *Roll of Thunder, Hear My Cry*. It is a long book, and I didn't want them to just dutifully creep through it. While waiting for the club members to assemble, Fallon explained to me, "Personally, I notice that I am trying to keep track of these characters because there are a bunch of them, and Stacey is a boy, not a girl. So it's a little confusing right at first, but I'm trying to keep track of everyone."

Isaac had arrived in time to hear Fallon, and he concurred. "Me too. I know soon I'll figure out who's who, but now I'm just trying to picture them—you know, walking to school and all."

I nodded. In this complex book, they were wise to try to figure out the who, when, where, and why. I was glad that even though it had been almost a week since I taught a mini-lesson emphasizing that readers tack up the information almost as if on a mental bulletin board, that was exactly what these readers were doing as they launched into their third book in the unit. (They'd already read *Freedom Summer* and *The Gold Cadillac*).

I emphasized to the children that I loved that they were trying to get things straightened out. "It's like the book opens on page 1 and immediately pours a pile of characters and situations onto you right away. And the first page in this book even starts in the middle of an action, doesn't it. They're walking to school and having a conversation, aren't they?"

Fallon nodded, "Yeah, I felt like I was just eavesdropping and trying to figure out who these people are, where they are, and what's going on."

I laughed. "Remember when you were younger—not all that younger, but less sophisticated as readers— we used to teach you, 'If you start reading a book and it is confusing, give it up. Say, 'This is too hard for me.' Now you are older, and you are realizing it isn't that simple 'cause some books, like this one, are probably *meant* to be confusing at the start, right? You are *supposed* to be doing just what you are doing, and that's saying, 'Huh?' and 'Whoa, what is going on?' Now that you are older, you know that good readers don't get all our confusions cleared up right away. We need to be able to live in that state of not-sureness and to read on, knowing the fog will lift.

"Even though sometimes the books are meant to be a bit confusing at first, it is still important to read trying to figure things out. It's like what you learned about hard words. They are hard—they are supposed to be hard—but if you work at it, you can figure them out. That's the same now with the confusing parts of your books. They are confusing—you are supposed to be confused—but you are also supposed to be able to figure those parts out, by working on them.

"Can I give you a tool that I think can help you keep track of everything that's happening in your books?" The club members nodded, curious. I placed a strip of paper in the middle of their group. "This strip can hold your timeline for the story of the

Making Our Way Through Historical Fiction

- *Collect setting details. What kind of place is this? What does it feel like?*

- *Is trouble brewing? How is it changing? What feels important?*

- *Collect vital data about characters. Traits? Pressures on them? Problems they face? What drives them?*

- *What new understanding and historical information do you have?*

- *What is the sequence of events in the story, including jumps in time?*

- *Notice what's changing in the book. How are the characters' problems escalating? Has the setting or the mood shifted?*

- *Think about how characters are reacting differently to big events and what we can learn from this.*

"Do some jotting, recording a timeline of your story or some of your thoughts. In a minute, you'll have a chance to talk about your thoughts, but let's take a second first to have that conversation not in the air, but on paper."

After giving children three minutes to rehearse for their clubs, I said, "Gather with your clubs, and decide how you're going to go about organizing your talk time. Be sure that the club members who made timelines have a chance to bring those into the conversation. Other than that, how you go about talking is up to you."

book. You'll need to fill in the timeline as you read, but for now let's pretend you've done that already so that I can show you ways to use it. When you sit down to have your club conversation, at least for a bit, you can begin your meeting by each bringing a Post-it with you. The Post-its could represent what you think is the most important event (or two) from the part you have read since your last meeting."

To demonstrate how to use the tool, I said, "For example, we've all read Chapter 1 in *Number the Stars*, and if we were meeting to discuss this book, we could start by discussing what we each thought was the most important event or two of that chapter. I might say, "I think the most important event of Chapter 1 is that Kirsti has talked back to the soldiers. So I would jot that on a Post-it in preparation for our meeting." I jotted, "Kirsti talked back to Nazis. Why would she do that?"

"But, Aly, maybe you'd have a different idea. What do you think is the most important part of Chapter 1?"

Aly thought for a moment and then said, "I think it's that Annemarie stood up for Ellen and that Ellen backed up behind her. I'm not sure why, but I think that's the biggest part."

"So we'd go on just like this, gathering our ideas about what the most important events or two are from Chapter 1, and then we'd discuss *why* we think the moment we've chosen is so important. Then, after a few minutes (or maybe longer, depending on where you take the conversation), all of you as a club would decide what *the* two most important moments are that you want to hold onto from the first chapter, and you'd decide to add those, and only those, to your timeline." I pointed out that sometimes they'd add moments that didn't actually happen in this story but that were part of the back story for their characters, or for the place or the times. Of course, they'd need to figure out where the moments went on a chronological timeline.

"So try this work with your club book, with *Roll of Thunder, Hear My Cry.*"

I knew that when I met with the club next, which I assumed would probably be the next day, I would show the club members that they could layer their thinking about the important events with thinking, also, about how those events affect each of several main characters differently. I knew I'd eventually show them that they could make a representation of each character and then show each character's emotional temperature in response to each event. For example, they could first consider each event through the eyes of their main character, Cassie, progressing along the timeline and asking, "How does Cassie react to this? To this?" If Cassie was not in the scene, they could still ask, "Knowing Cassie and people during this time, how *would* she probably have reacted to this situation?"

Actually, as this work unrolled, the Freedom Fighters themselves would end up adding a new twist to it. As it turned out, they decided to think of the region above the timeline as good/happy and the region below it as bad/unhappy, and to put a Post-it for each character somewhere in the region above or below each event, thereby signifying how each character reacted to each event, with the location of the Post-its representing differences and similarities in characters' responses to events.

The power of this work was not in the activity itself, but in the conversation that it provoked. The concrete nature of the project kept this club on track, talking in text-bound ways that nevertheless allowed them to unearth important confusions and differences of opinion.

The concrete tool was a temporary scaffold. By the time the readers were deep into *Roll of Thunder, Hear My Cry*, I suggested they talk without working inside the confines of this tool or this ritual. But for a bit of time, this kept the club deeply engaged doing the work they needed to do.

But anyhow, for now, I knew that the club members would find that making timelines for complex historical fiction wouldn't be as easy as it

sounds. Try it yourself and you will see! When there are multiple main characters, often many of those characters seem to each follow their own plotline. For example, in *Number the Stars*, there is one timeline on which the story of Annemarie and Ellen's life together unfurls. There is another timeline, however, reflecting the life of another sister, now missing, and her boyfriend, Peter. For a bit, it feels as if that second timeline will be important to the story, but then this secondary timeline seems to peter out. Because I have read enough historical fiction books to recognize patterns in them, when the plotline involving Annemarie's sister and her fiancé, Peter, petered out, I was confident that the trail would not be lost for good and was not in the least surprised when this eventually became significant to the main plotline. Children, however, still need the experience of reading tons of historical fiction books and coming over time to trust there will end up being a reason why those subordinate plotlines exist.

Conferring with the Pioneers: Pushing Past Initial Questions to Discuss the Deeper Questions Lurking Beneath

When I pulled close to the Pioneers, Jasmine had risen to her feet with a great flourish and was commanding her groups' attention as she read from *Sarah, Plain and Tall*, MacLachlan's beautiful book about the mail-order bride who traveled from her home in Maine to the prairie where she was now living with Pa, whom she might soon marry, and his two young children. The club members and I had talked the previous day about the goals they had for their group and agreed that what they really needed was to bring books to life more. They'd interpreted this to mean adding interludes of drama into the midst of their book club, and clearly this was one of those interludes. Jasmine read,

"Can't swim!" exclaimed Sarah. "I'll teach you in the cow pond."

"That's for cows!" I cried.

But Sarah had grabbed our hands and we were running through the fields, ducking under the fence to the far pond. (Jasmine assumed the role of Sarah, grabbing an imaginary hand, turning as if to run until she a large cow stood in her way, which she shooed.)

"Shoo cows," said Sarah as the cows looked up, startled. She took off her dress and waded into the water in her petticoat. She dived suddenly and disappeared for a moment as Caleb and I watched. She came up, laughing.

Putting the book down, Jasmine said, "See, that proves my answer to the question. She is learning how to have fun. And they are like family to her now 'cause it says right here: 'she took her dress off.'"

"It's not *all* off," Malik qualified. "The petticoats were almost the same as dresses."

"Still, she is showing that they are her family. And Caleb, too. How Caleb made a big wave of water go in her face. He wouldn't do that to a grown-up who is not part of the family. So those are my answers to the question. That, and what you said, Malik, about how when she wrote her brother, she said *our* dune, not *their* dune."

The group was silent for a minute, long enough that everyone started to giggle a little, to look between each other as if to say, "Do you have something to add?" and to eye me, hoping for a lifeline. "You are at one of those impasses that almost any conversation gets into," I said. "Can you feel it? It's like you are all eyeing each other and thinking, 'What do

we say now?' These are the times when you kind of check your watch and think, 'How much longer do we have?' and you hope the answer is two minutes, right?"

The kids nodded, giggled a bit, and with a touch of defensiveness explained to me that they'd already talked about a bunch of details that made them think Sarah was homesick enough that she might return to Maine and others that had made them think she'd stay in the prairie. They pointed out a few Post-its that had launched big conversations the day before. *[Figs. V-6 and V-7]* They didn't want me to think the conversation had just lasted ten minutes or anything. Yesterday, as well as today, they'd been talking about the question of whether or not she would stay and marry Pa or not. But yes, it sort of felt like they all agreed that she'd probably stay and marry Pa. So the conversation was at a lull.

"We could find more reasons," Malik added, "'Cause, we were noticing in the beginning that Papa didn't sing and now he is, so their lives are getting better because of Sarah."

I could tell from the way Malik said this comment that the group had already discussed the point about Pa's singing, and Malik was just trotting the comment out now to impress me. So I took a big breath, thinking, "Here goes," and said, "That idea, Malik, about Pa starting to sing now, it does go in the 'Evidence That Sarah Will Stay' column in your 'Will She Stay? Go?' conversation. I get the feeling that you'd already put it there, though, before right this minute—that you had already discussed it. I'm mentioning that because often what happens when a group gets into one of these impasses where the group doesn't know what else to talk about, people simply repeat everything that's already been said. Jasmine could go right back and say, 'I think she's gonna stay because, I mean, she went swimming with them and it says "she came up laughing." She is having fun and that shows. . . .' You could all repeat whatever you have already said, over and over until I say, 'Clubs, it is time to stop.'

"But here is my point. Once you have thought a lot about one question, if that question is central to the book, then usually the wisest thing to do is to see if you can dig deeper into that question. And the way to do this is to come up with another, more specific question, and usually the next question will be 'How?' or 'Why?' or 'So what?' or sometimes, 'What's the hard thing about this?'

"You willing to try it?" I asked. The kids nodded. "So let's assume that you've read up to page 37, and you've determined that Sarah will end up

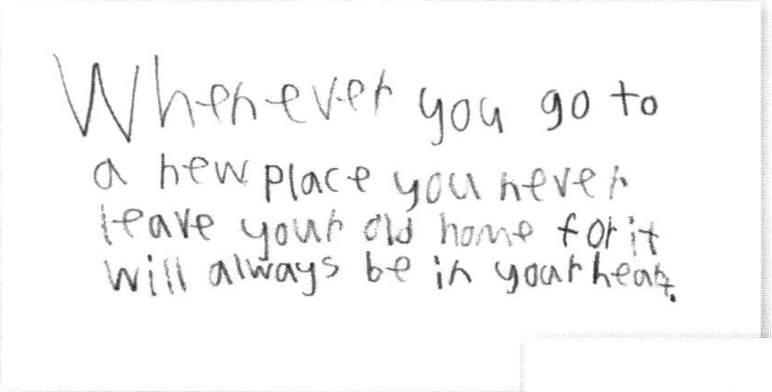

Whenever you go to
a new place you never
leave your old home for it
will always be in your heart.

Figure V-6

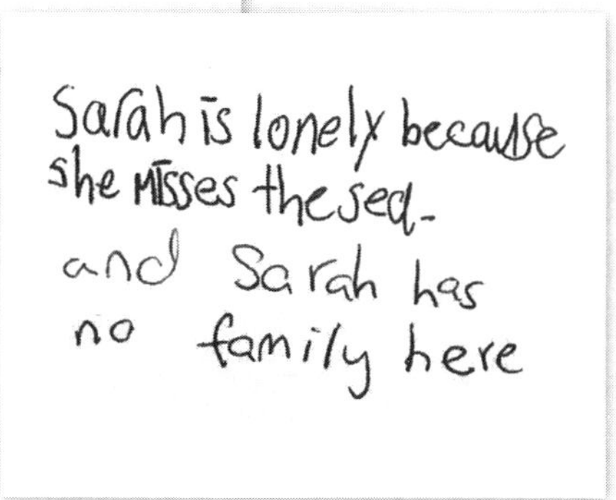

Sarah is lonely because
she misses the sea.
and Sarah has
no family here

Figure V-7

staying to marry Pa and become part of the family. She is lonesome for Maine, but she'll decide to stay and join this family anyhow. Now let's try to ask deeper questions about this, including questions of how, why, so what, and what's the hard thing about this. You can't just say a one-word question, though. You need to make it specific to this book. So jot some questions, specific to this book, that grow out of the feeling that she will probably stay and marry Pa. What are you still wondering?"

As the children wrote, I scanned their jottings. Then I said, "Let's talk in pairs about one of these questions that seems especially interesting. Once children primed the pump a bit and got some conversations going, I asked them to convene and to settle on one question that they'd discuss together. Soon the group had decided to talk about, "How will she feel? Will Sarah *still* be lonely, deep down?"

"Yeah," Lily said, flipping through the book. "Sarah says she misses William and her aunts. And before, when we first started reading this,

remember how we talked about when Sarah first came, she looked lonely. Remember, we thought she was already lonely even though she had only been there for like two minutes. I wrote 'Sarah is lonely because she misses the sea' here. The sea is like Sarah's friend, and now she is in a place without a sea."

"Yeah, but she likes the dad and the kids. And she likes the animals. The chickens." Malik said.

Kobe grinned at Malik. "Yeah, she even named those chickens."

"She also made a new friend," Jasmine added. "Maggie, the lady who came with her husband to help with the fields."

"Yeah," Lily said, "She is making new friends, and that makes me think she won't leave. She's . . ." Lily struggled to find the right word. "She's kind of getting attached."

At this point, I chimed in. "Do you notice that you asked a new question—Will Sarah still be lonely?—but your talk is sort of the same as it was, only now instead of listing reasons why she might stay or go, you are listing reasons why she might still be lonely or not. It doesn't feel to me that your new round of talk is getting much deeper. Instead, it feels sort of like the talk you had before, only I wonder even if there is any real question on the table. I mean, don't you think it is sort of obvious that although there will be things to love, she'll still miss what she has lost?" The kids nodded. "When you find that happening—when you are talking about something that feels sort of obvious—then you need to ask, 'What is the *real* question here?' What do you think the real question is. Is it, 'Why is she so lonely?' Is it, 'How will she ever get over the loneliness?' or what?"

The children decided they'd think about why Sarah felt such intense loneliness. With this question in hand, they agreed to read on. As I moved on from this group, I noted to myself that sometimes I can produce what I think is splendid advice, and it doesn't actually yield what I hoped for. Onward.

TEACHING SHARE

Readers Listen "Like Gold"

Ask your students to look around the room and notice how others are participating in club work, and then encourage them to look and act like engaged, caring readers.

After children talked for a bit, I said, "Will everyone freeze right exactly where you are? While not moving—just turning your head a tiny bit—look around the room and notice the way people in different clubs are sitting or standing. Who seems to be sitting in a listening way, regarding what club mates are saying as if it's gold? Who seems—from posture alone—to be acting like a curmudgeon when it comes to taking in other people's ideas?

"We already know that for a club to go well, the members need to take care of it. A big part of this involves making a commitment to really listen to each other. In this unit, you are going to be tackling really complex texts and doing some more sophisticated thinking. So I'm going to ask you to make a real commitment to doing that. I'm going to admire you now, as you do your best to really look and act like readers who care for each other as well as for the book." The children resumed their club conversations.

After a few minutes, I said, in a stage whisper, "Readers, freeze just where you are. I don't want to mess up a bit of this. It is so gorgeous. Right now, without turning your head, can you shift just your eyes a tiny bit so you see what this room looks like? Let's remember this sort of talking, this sort of listening, this sort of positioning when we are in our clubs tomorrow. So that we never forget this image, let's add 'Listen to conversation like it's gold' to our chart."

Growing Powerful Book Club Conversations

- Be a good listener by leaning in, making eye contact, and letting the person speaking finish his or her thought. You can even jot notes as someone speaks, to honor his or her words.

- Be aware of any member who has gone unheard. Invite him or her in.

- Listen to conversation like it's gold.

Great talk LOOKS like...
- citing the text (going to it)
- looking over post its and notes
- turning toward one another & making eye contact
- taking turns
- leaning in

Great talk SOUNDS like...
- "I see what you mean, but..."
- "That might be true, however..."
- thinking about all possibilities
- staying on one idea by responding to each other
- comparing mysteries/books
- arguing & disagreeing "I disagree..."

Thinking As Someone Else

IN THIS SESSION,
you will teach your students
that to deepen understanding of characters, readers
step into their shoes and
realize that they are shaped
by the times in which they
live.

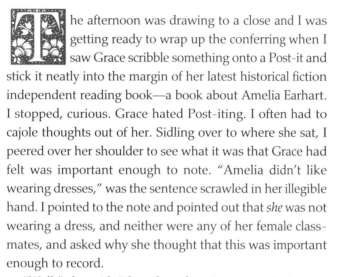

The afternoon was drawing to a close and I was getting ready to wrap up the conferring when I saw Grace scribble something onto a Post-it and stick it neatly into the margin of her latest historical fiction independent reading book—a book about Amelia Earhart. I stopped, curious. Grace hated Post-iting. I often had to cajole thoughts out of her. Sidling over to where she sat, I peered over her shoulder to see what it was that Grace had felt was important enough to note. "Amelia didn't like wearing dresses," was the sentence scrawled in her illegible hand. I pointed to the note and pointed out that *she* was not wearing a dress, and neither were any of her female class-mates, and asked why she thought that this was important enough to record.

"Well," she said, "*these days* almost everyone just wears pants. So me wearing pants doesn't matter. But when Amelia Earhart was a kid, it was really weird that she wanted to wear pants. Girls all wore dresses. It shows that she was different from other girls even when she was a kid." It is moments like this that teach us to stop and really listen

to our kids. Grace's illegibly scrawled five-word sentence inspired this minilesson.

Throughout the year, we have taught our students to empathize with the characters in their books. We've wanted them to be with Willy, racing across the moonlit snow faster, faster, faster, snowflakes blinding their eyes just as they blind Willy's. We've wanted our students to stand with Rob in the rainy morning, looking for that patch of yellow to show that the bus has turned the corner and is approaching. We've wanted them to enter that school bus with Rob, eyes downcast, hoping to get past the Threemonger bullies unnoticed. We've hoped our students are worrying when their characters are worrying and feeling hope swell in their chests when their characters are hoping. We have talked a lot about the value of walking in the shoes of a character and seeing the world through that person's eyes.

But now we hope that readers are able to do this not by bringing characters into their world but rather by allowing reading to transport them to the world in which the story takes place. And this means learning to assume perspectives

---

GETTING READY

- In the active involvement, you'll need examples from *Number the Stars* or a familiar text of times when a character has acted in a way that might at first seem surprising but becomes understandable when readers consider his or her historical context.

- During the teaching share, you will add to the "Growing Powerful Book Club Conversations" chart.

different from one's own, including imagining the effect of living in a different time and place. It will take a thoughtful, informed imagination for readers of Deborah Wiles's beautiful historical fiction picture book, *Freedom Summer*, a civil rights story set in the South during the late 1950s or early 1960s, to step into the shoes of the older brother, Will, an African American teenager, who is part of a work crew. On the day after Will and his family hear the joyous news that the town pool will at long last be open to everyone, black and white alike, that work crew is brought to the town pool and given the job of filling that pool, replacing the beautiful sparkling water with black, oozing tar. Will stands above the

> ## It's our job to help readers see behaviors and choices that bear noticing.

dump truck, shoveling the steaming goo into the pool, closing the pool to all rather than letting it become integrated. Will's little brother watches with big eyes from behind the bushes, and so does the reader. Most young readers will at first recoil and say, "I would never ever in a million years do that. How could Will do that? How could he?" Learning to read historical fiction well involves learning to answer that question. Yes, indeed, how could he? What does that most awful action show about the times? Reading involves walking in a character's shoes when it is agony to do so, when the act of imagination is tortuous.

But until now, we may not have acknowledged that sometimes walking in the shoes of another character involves assuming perspectives that are totally contrary to the reader's own perspective, understanding that those perspectives are situated in contexts utterly unlike the reader's own context. And that is why Grace's entry was so important.

What Grace intuitively understood is that truly standing in a character's shoes means that our own behaviors and preferences are not always the most useful barometer. We are all, in part, a product of our circumstances. A person's behaviors and actions can only be understood when considered in the context of that person's unique situation. Choices that would be unremarkable for someone in our time—wearing pants, for instance—*are* noteworthy when made by another person, in another time.

In this minilesson, students will learn the importance of examining their characters' actions through the lens of historical context. Characters in historical fiction texts often make choices that our students might dismiss by simply saying, "I would never do that!" How important it is for the reader to also say, "I wonder what was going on that played into this character's decision to do that?"

Then, too, characters in historical fiction make choices and take actions that might seem utterly unremarkable when regarded through the lens of our time today but that were actually brave, defiant decisions. Characters learn to read, stand up to their parents, wear pants, make a friend of a different background—choices that would be perfectly normal for most of our students to make today but might be breathtakingly important actions when considered within the setting of their times. It's our job to help readers see behaviors and choices that bear noticing. These are the choices that reveal the essential nature of a character and of the world, too, and these choices provide clues about what's to come for that character and that world down the road. The choices sometimes portend the character's contribution to progress.

We hope that this skill will transfer to students' lives outside of the reading workshop. We will be looking for such instances, and when we notice them we will make a point of drawing the class's attention to them. Whether using examples from the classroom or from the news, we will take every possible opportunity to help students hone their awareness of others' circumstances.

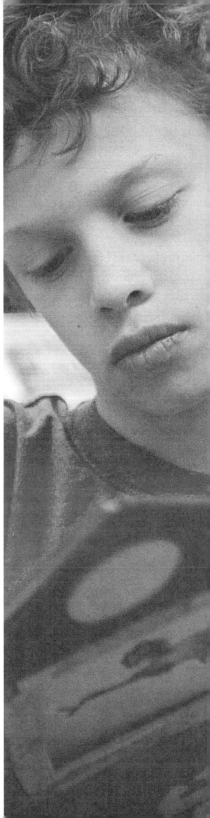

MINILESSON

Thinking As Someone Else

CONNECTION

COACHING TIPS

Compare the way you have gotten to know children to the way readers get to know characters. Explain, too, how a reader's understanding of characters changes as the reader learns about the historical context in which the story is set.

"Readers, it seems like such a long, long time ago, now, but at the end of last school year, our principal gave me a list of children who would be in our class this year. That's all I had—just a list of names. I had seen a couple of you in the hallways, so I had some idea of what your faces looked like. Over the summer and in the days before the first day of school, as I prepared for our year together, I wondered to myself what you would be like. As I wrote your names on your Reading Life folders, I wondered, 'Is Tyrell going to be loud or quiet?' 'Will Fallon like music or gym?' As I made up our first seating chart, I tried to imagine personalities just by the sound of your names, because that is all I had to go on. I figured Grace would be really into science and would have pockets full of little machines and technological tools and maybe creatures, too.

"Then, we had our first day together, remember? And you all gathered here with your faces scrubbed and gleaming, like shiny pennies. I learned a few things about you that first day. For instance, I learned that Brianna loves soccer. You were even carrying your cleats to school that day! Then, over the next days and weeks, I learned so much more about you. I learned about your families, and the things that you enjoy, and the things you struggle with, and the kind of friends you are to each other and to me. Bit by bit, I learned about your dreams for yourselves and your quirky personalities. You're not just names on a list to me anymore.

Making your own ponderings about what your students would be like as detailed as possible will not only engage them in your lesson immediately—who doesn't love to hear details about themselves—but it also subtly models the detailed thinking you will want your students to do about their characters.

Even though you are teaching a reading minilesson, you are also constantly tucking in messages about the importance of the classroom community. Your teaching, hopefully, reminds children that they are not just in book clubs, but they are also in one big club of classmates.

"This is how we get to know characters in books, too. They start off as names on the page, and then as we read, we get to know the choices they make, the background stories that leak out, the things they carry. Everything we learn about a person goes into our composite sense of that person. Meeting the person, whether in life or on the page, is just the start of a long process. Bit by bit we uncover more and more layers. We learn the outer persona, and then we learn the person underneath that outer persona, behind the face she puts on for the world. We learn what she hopes for and fears, who she is when she's alone and when she's in the company of others. If we are lucky, we come to understand the person.

"When reading historical fiction, we have these extra layers of information that shed light on our characters' behaviors and motivations. We have the history surrounding the time period and world in which the character lives. We can ask, 'How do the historical events in this character's world influence her decisions? How do her status and privileges—or lack of these—influence how she acts, the choices she makes?'"

Tell the story of a child who tried to make sense of his character's choices by considering the historical backdrop in his book.

"Readers, the other day I was listening in as one club, The Dust Bowl, discussed the part of *Bud, Not Buddy* in which Bud, who is only ten years old, plans to sneak onto a passing cargo train so he can move to a new town. Kwami said, 'I think Bud is sort of a bad kid, because he should be going to school, not jumping on trains.'

"Then Jack said a smart thing. He said to Kwami, 'I disagree because remember, this story takes place in the Depression, when lots of people were dying, they were so poor. I don't think Bud is goofing off just because he's not at school. I mean, he's trying to find his father. I think he is doing the grown-up thing.'

How important it is to show children that reading historical fiction (and indeed all complex fiction) involves charting the big picture, such as that comprised of historical events that occur on a large scale and are recorded by newspapers and books, and drawing out the smaller stories in the lives of the people—people like the Rosens and the Johansens. These smaller stories are the kind of stories that are often unreported, unwritten by historians. Only rarely do we get to know what history felt like through the eyes and hearts of those who lived through it, but historical fiction gives us an idea of what this must have been like. You could say, in a way, that historical fiction brings history to life.

As I reference a particular book, I try to have a copy of the text in my hand to show the class. They can see the title and the cover illustration, which I gesture to as I make my point. This is a simple way to make our teaching more concrete and visual for those children who find it a challenge to internalize our teaching from spoken language only.

Whenever you have a conference with a reader or club that might benefit the majority of your readers, turn it into a minilesson. The readers who have already heard the teaching point will be delighted that you are using them as an example, and the rest of the class will enjoy hearing a story about their peers. All of this lifts the level of engagement.

"Listening, I thought, *wow*. It is great to read, being aware of the historical times in which a story is set (I put out one arm), and great to read, being able to retell the personal timelines of the main characters (I put out the other arm). But to put those two together—to suggest that the one timeline interweaves and affects the other (I twisted my arms, then held up a piece of cord made from two colors twisted together), that this twisted-togetherness helps us explain why characters behave the way they do, that is brilliant!"

Name your teaching point. Specifically, tell children that when readers get to know the characters in our historical fiction books, we step into the period in which they live, and we try to see the world through the eyes of someone in their times.

"Readers try to understand the decisions that characters make, and we do this in part by keeping in mind that the character's behavior is shaped by what is happening in the world in which the character lives, that is, by the historical context. And here's the thing: When different characters respond differently to one event, it is helpful for readers to muse about this, asking 'Why?' Usually when different characters act differently this reflects the fact that each of those characters plays a different role in the world and therefore is shaped differently by the times."

Teaching

Ask your readers to reconsider a familiar scene from your read-aloud, thinking this time about *why* characters behave the way they do, including thinking about the historical context that shapes each of them.

"Readers, I'm going to revisit a familiar scene from the first chapter of *Number the Stars*. I want to show you how I notice characters' behaviors and try to make sense of them in terms of what I understand about the context of their lives. Remember the moment when the German soldier orders, '*Halte!*' as Annemarie and Ellen are running and laughing down the street? Annemarie says that she found that word familiar and frightening. Yes, she said 'frightening.'

If you don't have a cord that illustrates the weaving together of two timelines, you might use something else you have in the classroom—a child's lanyard keychain or even a student's braid. If necessary, try roping your right and left arms together. It can really help to make your metaphor visual.

This is a long and complex teaching point. You can be sure I reread it five times, trying to trim and tighten it. Teaching points should be easily said and easily remembered. This one isn't. But this is crystal clear, and every word feels important, so I wasn't able to find a way to revise it. If your children are third graders, you'll probably delete the last point, leaving that to another day's minilesson or to your mid-workshop teaching point or your share.

Teachers, investigating characters' motivations for their behaviors becomes increasingly complicated as the books your children are reading become more complex. Characters in these stories experience pressures from many sources. Some will be personal, and some will be related, in historical fiction, to the pressure of historical events. Ultimately, we want our students to be able to temporarily put aside their own history and imagine the history of the characters in their stories. We want them to think hard about the perspectives of these characters, about what influences their points of view, about why they do the things they do. This is another example of how historical fiction carries readers into reading work that will, ultimately, help them in complex texts in any genre.

"When we first read this part, I found myself thinking that Annemarie must be easily frightened, if she finds the word *stop*, or *halte*, frightening. After all, I thought, it makes sense to be embarrassed if you are told to stop running by a guard, but it's ridiculous to be frightened. Guards are there to keep children safe.

"Readers, in my mind, I was imagining the crossing guards and policemen that I'm familiar with, and I was picturing how friendly we are with the people who patrol our streets and keep kids out of traffic and trouble. But now I'm realizing that I wasn't really imagining Annemarie's perspective. Instead, I was inserting *my* perspective into the story. I was seeing things through the lens of *my* experiences.

"Let's see what happens when I reconsider this scene, really trying to imagine *Annemarie's* perspective, including the historical context that shapes her thinking. Well, to Annemarie, these aren't friendly neighborhood guards. They are soldiers from an enemy army, who have occupied her town. They carry guns. In fact, it said in this part that they had 'two sets of cold eyes.' These soldiers aren't like the people who patrol our streets.

"Readers, I realize that it's going to be really important for me, and for all of us, to step outside of our own perspectives and really imagine the perspectives of the characters in these historical fiction stories. Especially if we find ourselves surprised by or perplexed by the characters' behaviors, chances are we may need to reconsider how the characters are shaped by the history that surrounds them."

Demonstrate that even in the same historical moment, characters' behaviors will be influenced by factors such as their age, their culture, and their social or political position.

"There's one more thing, though. Even when we examine one moment in a story, and we think about the particular historical events that may be influencing characters, there will still be differences among the characters. Characters will respond to the same situation differently, sometimes because of age differences or cultural differences or social and political differences. Let me show you what I mean." I picked up the book and made it clear that now I wasn't just recalling, I was reading the exact words.

I purposely chose to tell the story from a modern perspective such as this, which clearly does not fit with what we know about the historical context in which Annemarie was living. I'm hoping that students will already be thinking to themselves that my understanding of Annemarie's reaction doesn't make sense. I'm hoping that they will want to protest my assumption that guards are there to protect people by recalling what they now know about the German guards and Annemarie's situation in Number the Stars. *Often when I teach, my goal is not just to deliver new information to students but also to help them to identify and name something they've already been doing as readers. This helps them to recognize the work they have been doing in a way that they can hone and practice and in a way that is transferable to other texts and situations.*

I refer to the text often when I'm doing this kind of work with perspective. Because there are a multitude of ways to experience an event, I find it is so important to really use the text as an anchor to understand not only the historical events but also the character's reactions as they are explained in the text. Doing this work requires a delicate balance between making inferences about how and why the characters might react to certain events based on what you know about the character and the time period and reading the text very closely, looking for details that tell about a character's reaction. Working closely with the text in this way can also help readers to focus on the perspective the character, *not the* reader, *brings to events.*

You'll recall that I mentioned that the teaching point is a complex one, and the second half of it might be saved for a second minilesson. If you made that decision, this portion of your teaching could be moved to that new minilesson.

Ellen was motionless on the sidewalk, a few yards behind her. Farther back, Kirsti was still sulking, and walking slowly toward the corner. Nearby, a woman had come to the doorway of a shop and was standing silently, watching.

"These characters are all alive at the same time. They live in the same town. They are involved in the same incident. But I notice that they behave so differently, readers! Annemarie talks, Ellen seems frozen, Kirsti ignores everyone, and the woman watches. Once I notice that the characters behave differently, I ask myself, 'Why? What influences each of them?' I can't always answer a question like that right away. But as I read on, I'll be alert to anything that explains their behaviors. Perhaps Ellen has more reason to be fearful than Annemarie. Here's the thing, though, readers. Sometimes you have to wait, and more of the story will have to unfold, or you'll find out more through flashbacks or back stories. The main thing is that we notice that characters are reacting differently than we might in any situation, and we notice when individual characters respond differently. Next, we think deeply about the historical context and how that might be shaping characters' behaviors.

ACTIVE INVOLVEMENT

Remind children that we push past reactions toward our characters that reflect our own experiences instead of our characters' unique place in history.

"Readers, let's investigate *your* responses to this part of the story. When many of you read that German soldiers ordered the girls to stop, you protested. 'I wouldn't have stopped running down the sidewalk just because two soldiers told me to halt!' you said. But now I want you to reconsider. This time, remember that the German occupation of Copenhagen is not just something that occurred on that historical timeline. (I used my upright arm to suggest a distinct timeline.) It is something that winds in and out of the characters' lives, shaping their behaviors. The historical timeline stops Annemarie and Ellen in their tracks as those Germans call, '*Halte*!'

"Let me remind you, it is wise to think, 'I wonder *why* Annemarie responded like that? What *could be* the reason?' It is wise to think about the times, the *context* in which the story is set, and to think about the particular character's role in those times."

When I suggest I am unsure why Ellen reacts differently than Annemarie to the soldiers, I'm not being entirely truthful. I know full well that Ellen is Jewish, so her interpretation of these events comes from an entirely different perspective. Because that answer is so readily accessible, I do not want to be the one to produce it. By articulating the question and suggesting that we might read on to try to figure out an answer, I am setting children up to have success doing this work. If I'm going to demonstrate, I try not to take the easier bit of work for myself.

Set children up to think across one event from the perspective of multiple characters, all of whom have different reactions because of their different positions toward the central issue in the book.

"Let's look at that time when the soldiers stopped the girls in their tracks. Think right now, 'How does Annemarie react to the soldiers?'" I left a pool of silence as I thought about that myself. "How about Ellen? Kirsti?" Again I left a pool of silence. "How about Mrs. Rosen?" Again, I did the thinking I was asking children to do, leaving space for the children to do the same. "Now, here is a big question. What do you make of those different reactions?

"Here is a tip. When a person wants to understand a bit more about how different characters react differently to an event in history, it helps to ask, 'Where does he or she stand on the central issue in the book?'

"As you think about Annemarie's reaction to the soldiers, and Ellen's, and Ellen's mother, keep in mind the question, 'How do each of these individuals stand in relation to the central issue of this book?' That issue is probably the persecution of the Jews. So think, 'Where do they stand in relation to that issue, and how might this explain the differences in their responses?' For example, why was Mrs. Rosen so devastated that she had to stop having coffee and to retreat to her apartment? Why was Kirsti totally unaffected by the event? Turn and talk with your clubs about this."

Summarize the children's thinking, helping students understand that characters' reactions are linked to their identities and membership in various groups and their position in historical contexts.

After children talked, I repeated what a few of them had said and then summed up the work, saying, "Here is the important thing for you to understand. Characters in a historical fiction story—and in any story—are not just individuals. Like people the world over, a character is someone who belongs to a whole bunch of different groups. I am not just myself, an individual. I am also a daughter and, more specifically, the daughter of two doctors. I am a dog owner. I am a writer. All those things influence my reactions to events—just like Mrs. Rosen's membership in the group of Jewish mothers during the Holocaust effects what she sees."

It is impossible to emphasize enough the importance of you taking in the words that you are saying! You could rattle through this little paragraph, for example, and it could roll right over your kids (and you.) But listen to this point. It is absolutely huge. What could be more important than teaching kids the value of trying to see the world through the eyes of someone different than themselves? And how could a child ever be a thoughtful reader of history or of anything, really, if the child does not learn to do this? Yet the vast majority of kids will enter your classroom saying, in a very glib fashion, "I would never do that. I would never eat a caterpillar. I would never pretend to not know my own brother. I would never let soldiers make my friend and me stop running down the sidewalk." The truth is that life isn't so simple, and learning to read complex texts has a lot to do with learning to deal with the complexities of life.

Of course, there are pretty obvious reasons why Mrs. Rosen, a Jewish mother, is devastated to hear that German soldiers actually looked her daughter Ellen in the eyes, noticing her, accounting for her. And there are big reasons why five-year-old Kirsti, who has been shielded from the political drama, skips along without a care in the world.

It is significant, of course, that the encounter with the soldiers terrifies the parents. One reason that this affects Annemarie so differently than Kirsti is that Annemarie remembers how the city changed when the soldiers first arrived, while Kirsti thinks of the soldiers as a normal part of life because she doesn't remember a time before they were there. Although it is not hard to discern the reasons for the different perspectives, I want the children to feel as if they are accomplishing something incredibly complex when they recognize these different perspectives, because in fact the work they will be doing has the potential to be very complex and rich.

This event foreshadows what is to come. Mrs. Rosen believes that tensions are escalating, and of course, she is right to see the encounter as an ominous sign. This is an important part of the story to highlight because one of the major developments in the story is Annemarie's dawning understanding of the cruelty in the world around her. At one point in the story, a character makes the point that it is harder to be brave when you understand the risks. As Annemarie's understanding of the Nazis increases, so, too, does the pressure on her.

Link

Remind students that when characters act differently than we expect, it helps to ask why and to consider whether the context might play a part in this and whether a character's role or background might shape his or her response to events.

"Readers, I think we've all learned something really powerful that we can hold onto for the rest of our lives as readers. That is, when we read books about people living in times or situations that feel completely different from our own, we have to always take into account what influences were shaping *their* lives at that time. In the same way that some of us had to revise our initial reactions to Annemarie and Ellen stopping on command when the soldiers called out, '*Halte!*' because we now understood that they were living in a dangerous time, you will be doing the same things in your books as you read. It's too easy to say, 'She shouldn't have done that! He shouldn't have reacted that way!' because that is how *you* would have responded. We have to remember what our *characters* are living through, what kind of world our characters live in, and the kinds of places those characters inhabit in that world. We have to push ourselves to ask, 'Why would my character react that way?' and remember that a character is shaped as much by his or her history and background as we are.

"Here's the thing: When characters respond differently to one event, it is helpful for readers to muse about this, asking, 'Why?' Usually when characters act differently, this reflects the fact that each of those characters plays a different role in the world and therefore is shaped differently by the times."

Tell a personal story to show how our identities and backgrounds affect our reactions in a similar way as they affect characters in books.

"In fact, I was thinking of this very thing just last night because my dog was sick enough that she wasn't eating and seemed practically comatose to me. I was crazed over wanting to take her to the emergency veterinarian office. My husband said, 'Let's see how she is in the morning, and *then* if she's not okay, we can take her to our regular vet.'

It may be helpful, either in this session as a share or in a future session, to discuss some of the potential roles that people could have that might influence their responses to an event. Examples of such roles might be their age, gender, or race. It might be their position in their family. A mother might respond differently to a day of school being canceled because of snow than a child would, for example. Other roles might be someone's nationality or education level, or certainly, in the case of Annemarie, religion. If your students are older and a bit more advanced, they may be able to come up with pretty sophisticated roles to add to this list.

Of course, my membership in the club of people who write and in the club of people who teach also means that as events occur in my life, I watch them, and it is all grist for the mill. Teachers, like writers, are always spinning the flax of our lives into the golden threads of our teaching.

"There is a saying that when one goes over the bumps, what's inside spills out. When I thought about Emma's sickness and my husband's and my reactions to it, I realized that our histories and our backgrounds really affected the way we each responded. The way I reacted to Emma's sickness wasn't just a reflection of my personality, but also of my background. I am the daughter of two doctors and believe in the power of medicine. My husband, on the other hand, did not grow up with doctors and doesn't trust that rushing to a doctor will fix much. My membership in a family of doctors shaped *my* reaction just as strongly as my husband's membership in a family that didn't always trust doctors shaped *his*. Our behaviors are influenced by our histories, in life and in the books we read."

It is precisely true that as I wrote this portion of this minilesson, my dog lay at my feet, terribly sick, and my heart pounded as I wrote. I think that bringing my dog into the minilesson—a minilesson that has nothing to do with dogs—is important. You won't tell children about my dog, of course, but instead, you'll draw on the details of your own life. This is more important than you may realize. When you talk or write from the true stuff of your own life, there is something in your voice, your words, that catches people's attention and that creates an intimacy and an immediacy that makes your teaching and your relationships alive. It is a good discipline, then, to think about whatever is actually or metaphorically lying at your feet as you plan your teaching and to think, "So how can I somehow bring that into the teaching" I'm planning to do today?"

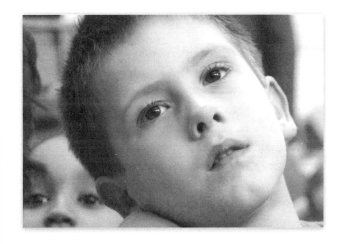

CONFERRING AND SMALL-GROUP WORK

Confer with Clubs Struggling with Hard Texts

In this session, your children will read as usual, and you'll confer as usual. This mid-workshop teaching point interrupts that reading. The visual layout of the page reflects the fact that well after the mid-workshop, readers will work in clubs and my discussion of conferring is situated within those clubs.

MID-WORKSHOP TEACHING POINT

Readers Think in Complex Ways About Characters' Motivations and Actions

"Readers, I want to remind you that whenever we read, we think deeply about the characters in our stories in terms of their personalities and relationships as well as their position in a historical context. For instance, when we're thinking about Annemarie confronting the soldiers and Ellen staying back, we can not only surmise that Annemarie feels more safe in this town, but we may also notice, as we're reading, that Annemarie seems to dominate this friendship. Characters have their own quirks, which we come to recognize as also shaping their behaviors. So when we analyze characters, we actually consider both the historical pressures they experience *and* their own personalities and inner flaws and strengths.

"When I think about how Annemarie first races down the street, for instance, I recall that it was Annemarie's idea. In fact, she had to persuade Ellen. She definitely seems like the more decisive girl

in this friendship. I also notice that while Annemarie seems very loyal to Ellen, she leaves Kirsti behind in the dash from school. She doesn't seem as fond of her own sister as she is of her friend. I know some people are like that. This definitely doesn't seem like something that was shaped by history. Girls choosing their friends over their sisters feels like something that could happen in any family, any time.

"Do you see how I did that? I thought back to a moment that at first seemed like such an important 'historical' moment: girls being frightened by German soldiers. But then I reconsidered how there was also a lot going on in that moment that was reflective of Annemarie's essential personality.

"As you carry on, keep in mind that your characters' behaviors in the book you are reading may be shaped by their personalities as well as by any historical context.

"Think of this as a new strategy to fit into your toolbox."

Coaching Clubs to Make Sense of Hard Texts Collaboratively

There's always the danger that our readers, when they encounter hard parts, will just blow through them, simply letting go of the parts of the story that they haven't worked to make sense of. If they keep reading, after all, something else will happen that perhaps does make sense. It's going to be important, therefore, to hold readers to the essential skill of monitoring for how all the parts of the story are making sense, and this will be especially important for any readers who are reading books that may be a bit hard for them. When the books get hard, readers need to work harder. Sometimes it even takes the combined effort of a group of readers to make sense of a story. If you've been reading adult historical fiction with your colleagues, you'll probably have found this. There will have been parts of the story that you had to retell, and revisit, together to make sense of them.

If a club of readers is reading books that are a bit hard for them, show them how the members of the club can work together to help each other keep track of the story line and to monitor for sense. With my Dust Bowl readers I decided to do just this, to nudge them toward reading with absolute alertness to the story line. I had a dual purpose in this. First of all, I knew that the books they would read, particularly *Out of the Dust*, are difficult, even for these fluent readers. Rather than blow through these books quickly, which is a bad habit that some strong readers develop, I wanted this club to read as if they had antennae up, constantly reaching out and taking stock of comprehension. I knew that the members of the club and I would have to all be working together to help them keep track of the story line and to monitor for sense. I had done a heavy book introduction with this club, and I planned to do another introduction part way through the book.

The goal of monitoring for sense might seem oddly low level to you, and you may think, "Isn't that more apt to be a goal at the start of the year?" That is true, but when children read books that are a bit challenging for them, then you will want to rally them to do the same skill-work that you stressed at the start of the year. So yes, you'll remind readers that it can help to pause after reading a chunk of text (perhaps a chapter or two) and to make sure that they have straight in their minds who is doing what, where, how, and why. The who, what, where, when, and why questions are easy to ask, but actually maintaining a coherent understanding of a complex text can be extremely challenging. I'll never forget that when my friends and I read *Beloved* together, we began each book club meeting by simply trying to construct the story line together. We'd do a shared "Previously in . . ." retelling each time we met, and during that retelling, we often were not sure of what exactly *had* occurred in the book, so we'd open the text to places that were confusing and reread them, trying to get our bearings. We learned that a collaborative retelling would often help each of us fill in parts of our understanding that had been shaky.

Of course, if your readers who are working with challenging texts are reading books that are at levels R and beyond, as The Dust Bowl readers were, they'll need to be reminded that if the book seems confusing, this may be because the author wants them to be confused. These texts are often constructed like a puzzle, and readers are supposed to struggle to figure out how the different puzzle pieces go together. They may need to

hold a confusing part in mind and read on, trusting that in time that part will snap into place with the rest of the story. Your hope is that you'll be able to convince these readers to reread the book they are reading so they realize, in a second read, the way the pieces of the text all fit together and so they realize, too, how many more layers the story has than that which they've been following.

My second goal in underscoring the importance of reading with "antennae up" was to help these readers take comprehension to a higher level. These readers bought into the idea (which I had planted) that their reading needed to be more attentive, more alert. I had rallied these readers to watch especially for ways that the author conveys significance, imbuing what could be everyday details with added layers of meaning.

These club members, high-level, fluent readers all, had even been convinced to do some rereading, and to do so in an effort to notice all that they zipped right past in their first read. I could provide plenty of real-life examples from my own real-life reading life that described how I'd have missed crucially important details if I hadn't gone back to reread. The club members were now Post-iting places where an image or a phrase reoccurred, suggesting significance. It seemed to be that over time, club members were beginning to notice when the author had used a certain style of writing to somehow convey, "This matters," like how in *Bud, Not Buddy* Christopher Paul Curtis often refers to the main character's "rules and things" to show that, as one club member, José, said, "Even though he doesn't have grown-ups telling him what to do, he still wants to have rules to follow." Moreover, I knew that as these readers tackled *Out of the Dust*, a book written as a series of chronologically ordered poems, paying attention to this sophisticated text would be critical to developing ideas.

This club, like the Freedom Fighters Club, which was attending to multiple plot lines, might also have been channeled to use all that they noticed to make predictions, but for this club, the most pressing question was, "What is this author trying to say about life and the world? And if that is what the author is trying to say, how will the story unfold?" Best of all, with a little nudging from me, the members of those two clubs "had the idea" to spend some time teaching each other some of the cool ideas for ways of working that they invented (or learned from me and thought they had invented), thus doubling each club's repertoire.

A Multifaceted Approach to Building Fluency

You might find that it is beneficial to actually sit with a club and help them make a plan for their reading schedule over the next week. For example, checking in on the Civil War Club, a club I knew had been thinking about volume already and had been using (with moderate effect) a stopwatch to help them read more during school reading time, I thought it might help for them to have more of a long-range set of reading goals and to be more specific about how many pages they should be reading with each reading session. I pointed out to them that they are expected to read *at least* half an hour a night, but that figure is a minimum one. This was their goal, but they'd want to reach for a way higher number than that. If they'd be read-

ing forty-five minutes, then that meant they could read at least thirty-five pages in one night, and almost the same amount in school the next day. As I set this up, I found that both Tyrell and Gabe were suddenly chomping at the bit to read more, and I set them up with a similar schedule through independent reading books.

I knew the members of this club had gotten into a pattern of reading selected passages aloud to each other. I wanted to hear this oral reading, and especially to check in on their work with a passage containing complex punctuation. It wasn't hard to scan through the pages the group had been reading in *Freedom's Wings* and to find a passage that had lots of interesting punctuation and heated emotions. In a conference, I asked the club members to try their hand at reading that passage aloud. I noticed immediately that, as I suspected it might, their fluency got bogged down in part by a preponderance of unfamiliar words. The terms weren't necessarily super hard—words like warbler and kettle—but they were unfamiliar words and therefore required a bit of extra time.

In this case, I decided to give an introduction to an upcoming chapter to help them be less bogged down with the unfamiliar terminology. I quickly skimmed through, picked out, and pretaught them some words and then suggested that it is really important for the kids to become accustomed to using those words. Sometimes children like to create their own little book-specific word banks, even just on an index card. The important thing is that you'll want to encourage them to actually use the new words in conversations about the book. So instead of saying, "Corey's dad is teaching him bird songs," a child might deliberately say, "Corey's dad is teaching him to make the songs of the warbler and the bobwhite."

Of course, you will not always be with children to introduce new terminology to them, so you may want to hand over your role, showing them that they can, in fact, assume the teacher's job, looking over a passage before they read it to extract a short list of potentially difficult words. The group then could work as a team to try to at least categorize the words. One list of words might be things found on the plantation; another might be words associated with the birds Corey is learning about. When we've invited youngsters to preview their upcoming text together and to work shoulder to shoulder to figure out some of the hard words, at least categorizing them into kinds of words, the energy this has produced has been remarkable, so make this suggestion as if you are sure it will be enormous fun for kids, as well as a way for young children to do exactly what we, as grown ups, do.

Of course, I wanted to balance help that was directed toward difficult terminology with help that kept the club invested in their goal to develop their fluency. In addition to the work I did helping members of the Civil War Club with vocabulary, then, I also suggested some "cool stuff" they could do within their club meetings. I said, "Do you remember how much fun it was when we were acting out how Rob stood there, under the sign for his motel, looking down the road for the bus? And we also acted out how he stood and took it when those bullies ground their knuckles into his scalp. The role-playing work we did back then really changed how I read books. It was sort of amazing for me because even if we just did five minutes in school of role playing, then I'd be lying on my bed at home reading, and I almost felt like I was still acting the scene out. But that really helped me to read with more feeling, with more expression. Is there any way you'd want to do that work now, in your clubs?"

If you suggest similar work with one of your clubs, I promise you, the kids will absolutely be game, and their work will keep them deeply engaged. When you're able to return to them, you'll be able to teach them to attend to punctuation, to work on phrasing, to use intonation to reflect meaning, and a million other lessons. But meanwhile, this existing endeavor, plus the emphasis on ramping up their volume of reading, will make a difference.

TEACHING SHARE

Readers Make Timelines to Help Them Think in Complex Ways

Remind your students that readers notice how characters respond differently to events in history, highlighting the work of a group that worked on this.

"Club members, we need to stop reading." Once I had readers' attention, I continued. "Let me tell you about some thinking that the Freedom Fighters did today. Earlier we talked about the fact that when we, as readers, notice that something big has happened in history (on the history timeline), it is unbelievably powerful to notice how characters respond *differently* to that one event, like we thought about when we saw that Ellen and Annemarie and Mrs. Rosen all responded differently to those Germans on the corner.

"Three things matter about the work the Freedom Fighters did today. One is that they were really trying to do the new work we took on as readers today. They decided to look closely at the daily life of the characters during the historical time period and place in their book, because they thought that would give them insight into understanding the characters. They were able to layer new work onto their ongoing work. They were already working on staying with one idea for long conversations, and they had already begun looking at daily life, but now they wanted to step out of their modern perspectives and really try to understand characters' behaviors and values by understanding the historical context."

Encourage students to use an easier text to practice new work, if necessary, and to root their conversations in one particular moment in a story.

"Here's the second thing they did, though, that will help all of us. When they found that this work was really hard to do in their new book (it's a hard book), they moved to practicing it in a familiar text, the picture book *Freedom Summer*. That is so smart, readers, to understand that when you try new, hard reading work, you want to try it first on a text that isn't also hard just on its own. So they moved back to *Freedom Summer*, which they knew inside and out.

"And here's the third thing the Freedom Fighters did: They launched their conversation by closely studying a specific page of the text, an incident in the book, so that they could use that page, and that moment, as the anchor for their conversation about daily life, historical context, and understanding character.

COACHING TIPS

Although a portion of my conferring and small-group work will usually be channeled toward mobilizing each club to pursue a clear agenda, on this particular day, I also invested some time in making sure today's minilesson had traction. It is one thing to tell children to read passages closely, annotating them, drawing information from them about the times and the characters' responses to the times, and it is another thing entirely for them to actually do this work.

It may seem as though I am complicating matters by highlighting more than one of this club's strengths, but each of the three things the Freedom Fighters did actually fits together to create their wonderful conversation. Sometimes it helps to highlight skills working together rather than in isolation.

Compliment club members for allowing disagreements to generate more thinking rather than shutting conversations down.

"I also want to call your attention to some strong work I heard in all the clubs today. I'm noticing that many of you are getting into heated conversations; sometimes you have different opinions or feelings about the characters and events in your books. And that's a good thing because it keeps the conversation moving. Strong conversations often grow out of that sort of passionate debate—so long as we stay open to different points of view. So instead of saying, 'No, that's not true,' we might say, 'That may be true, but I see it differently,' or 'Another way of thinking about that is. . . .' Let's add that to our chart on growing powerful book club conversations."

Growing Powerful Book Club Conversations

- Be a good listener by leaning in, making eye contact, and letting the person speaking finish his or her thought. You can even jot notes as someone speaks, to honor his or her words.

- Be aware of any member who has gone unheard. Invite him or her in.

- Listen to conversation like it's gold.

- Allow disagreements to generate more thinking. It can help to say, "That may be true, but I see it differently," or "Another way of thinking about that is. . . ."

When we disagree...

Instead of:	Try this:
You are wrong. That isn't how it happened.	I don't remember it that way. Can you show me that part?
I don't want to talk about that part.	Why would you want to talk about that part?
That doesn't make any sense.	

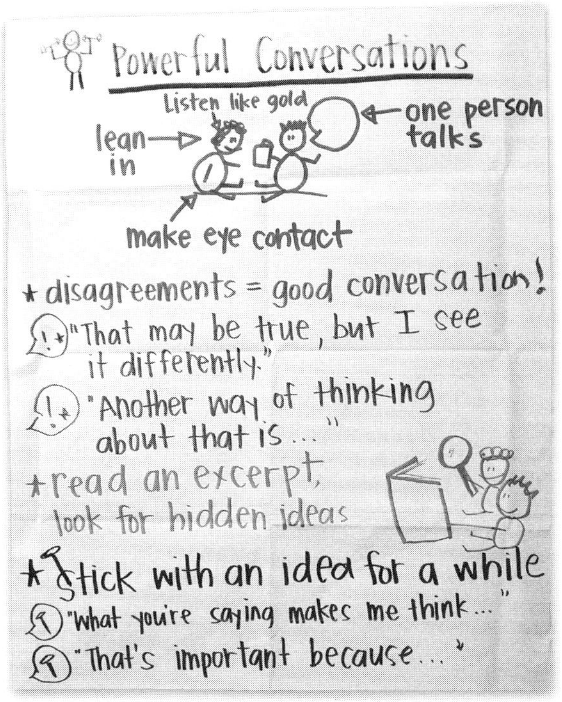

Powerful Conversations

Listen like gold
one person talks
lean in
make eye contact

* disagreements = good conversation!
"That may be true, but I see it differently."
"Another way of thinking about that is..."
* read an excerpt, look for hidden ideas
* stick with an idea for a while
"What you're saying makes me think..."
"That's important because..."

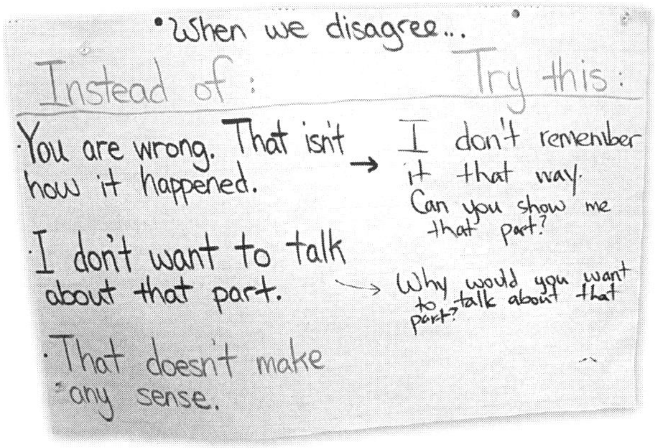

Scrutinizing, Not Skipping, Descriptions

ovice teachers worry, "What will I teach?" but once any of us has taught for even just a few weeks, we realize the real question is not "What *will* I teach?" but rather "What *won't* I teach?" Our hardest decisions will revolve around what *not* to teach. Now that both clubs and historical fiction reading are launched in your classroom, you'll no doubt feel as if everywhere you turn, you see more possible teaching points. You could teach a million tips about talking well in clubs. You could help children write to think so they grow ideas in preparation for a conversation. Because your children are now reading more complex books, you could teach them about monitoring for sense and dealing with difficulties.

I want, first of all, to encourage you to create your own minilessons out of any of those ideas, and especially out of the ideas that have resonance for you because of the reading you and your children are doing. There is nothing inevitable about the minilesson that Mary and I decide to teach next. You could easily postpone the minilesson we suggest, teaching first a few that are on the tip of your tongue.

That does not mean that we did not weigh competing priorities and decide on the upcoming session with some care. You'll see that we decided, in this session, to emphasize nose-in-the-book reading and the fact that readers need to make movies in the mind. We are hoping that this single minilesson will bring many prior minilessons back to

GETTING READY

- Expect that many of your clubs have finished at least one and perhaps two chapter books as well as a picture book by today. If any club is not well into its second chapter book, be ready to help them ramp up their volume of reading immediately.

- Be prepared to read parts of, but not all of, Chapter 3 of *Number the Stars* within this minilesson.

- This minilesson asks children to join you in close reading and annotation of the first page of Chapter 3. Ideally, have duplicates of just that page for each child to work on, or you could project the text on a screen or copy the paragraph onto chart paper. It is provided for you on the *Resources for Teaching Reading* CD-ROM.

- During the link, you will add to the "Making Our Way Through Historical Fiction" chart.

- Provide each club with a descriptive passage from that club's book that merits close reading, so that kids can use them for practice.

- During the teaching share, you will add to the "Growing Powerful Book Club Conversations" chart.

life—that it will be what we refer to as a repertoire minilesson, one that demonstrates to young readers that they have inside of them a repertoire of reading skills to draw upon. Now they need to activate them.

To show you what I mean, let me divert to the teaching of writing for a minute. Imagine this situation. You teach your writers a unit on revision, showing them four or five revision strategies they can use throughout life when revising their writing. Then it comes time for a unit on another

> *Young readers grow as they continue to use the same skills to make meaning with progressively more complex texts and in increasingly complex ways.*

topic—say, writing feature articles. The kids write a draft from beginning to end and then push it toward you, saying, "I'm done." They give no thought to revision. You need not reteach the entire original unit, but you can, instead, develop a repertoire minilesson that reminds kids to draw on their full repertoire of what they know how to do. That minilesson may tell kids they have an option as writers: Do they want to be dependent writers who throw their hands into the air and squeak out a needy "Help me. Help me," or do they want to be in-charge writers who sit up tall and think, "I know ways to revise. I can help myself." Within that repertoire minilesson, you could tuck a quick review of all the revision strategies you've already taught, but your real message is "Go at it. Writers use what we know."

In teaching reading as in teaching writing, we cannot simply assume that children will transfer all they learned in one unit of study to another. Explicitly teaching for transfer is critical because if readers don't transfer what they learned from one unit to the next one, the chances are not good that they'll transfer what they learned from school to their lives. If our goal is to affect what kids do for the rest of their lives, then it is essential that we move heaven and earth to be sure the lessons we taught in September and October shape what kids do in January and February! This does not mean that we'll reteach each and every minilesson as a self-standing new lesson situated in the new context. Instead, we should be able to devise minilessons that encourage our readers to draw on their full repertoire, using strategies they learned earlier with new flexibility and sense of purpose.

There is another reason why we've chosen to return to the familiar message that readers envision and predict by making movies in the mind. Growth in reading occurs along a spiral. Young readers grow as they continue to use the same skills to make meaning with progressively more complex texts and in increasingly complex ways. Although this session returns to the importance of envisioning, the work readers are asked to do to envision their historical fiction stories will be far more demanding than the work they needed to do when they were envisioning realistic fiction. They have to incorporate more details from the text. Because historical fiction stories are set in worlds that are different from our own, constructing mental images requires close reading. Then, too, when reading historical fiction, students not only need to imagine the world of the story; they must also think about how the nature of that world affects the characters within it. Historical fiction readers need to consider the atmosphere of this place as well as what it looks like.

Finally, we return to the familiar turf of envisioning because it is essential to keep in mind that children ultimately learn to read by reading. Our minilessons are nice additions to the curriculum, but the truly essential work is that which readers do as they sit with stories, making movies in their minds. Above all, our teaching needs to celebrate and to make a space for that work.

MINILESSON

Scrutinizing, Not Skipping, Descriptions

CONNECTION

Tell readers that in your own reading club, you are learning about club mates' reading quirks. Share some, suggesting that clubs are places to share such fun information.

"Readers, I don't know about you, but in the reading club that I've formed with other teachers, I'm finding out that some people do some really quirky stuff as readers. I have one club mate who literally reads *the endings* of books before she reads anything else! I have another club mate who *re*reads books *all the time*—as often as four or five times. Sometimes she can be three chapters into a book before she gets this vague feeling that the story is sort of familiar, that she's read it before. I have another friend who owns every single book written by her favorite author. She even belongs to his online fan club.

"I'm wondering if you have friends or club mates who do quirky things as readers? Try some true confessions in your clubs, 'cause you'll be surprised what some people secretly do. And book clubs should be places where we can share secrets, right?"

Tell readers that you, or a reader you've known, used to skip descriptive parts. Tell children that by reading with a friend who loved those parts and by reading historical fiction, this has changed.

"So I thought I'd tell you one of my reading secrets. I have one of those 'I used to be . . . , but now I am . . .' stories as a reader. This is it. I *used to* pretty much skip some parts of books. You know how there are fast-action parts of the book where people are coming and going, doing and saying stuff? I've always read *those* parts, and read them quickly 'cause I want to find out what will happen next. But then I come to those paragraphs—they are usually fat paragraphs written all the way to the edges of the page—where the author describes the place, telling about the curtains blowing in the wind of the open window and the moonlight falling on the empty rocking chair, and what not. Well, the truth is that I used to sort of *skip* those parts. I would skim them, just in

I had the hardest time starting this minilesson. I kept writing, "So far we have learned that readers take note of the vital statistics as we read. But I also want to teach you that. . . ." The problem was I was convinced that readers' eyes and minds would glaze over if I once again said, "So far we have learned. . . . Today I want to teach you. . . ." And no one wants our teaching to be dull! Instead, it needs to be worthy of the time it occupies. Think of it: Twenty-five children miss ten minutes of reading time to sit and listen to a minilesson. What a responsibility we have, then, to teach in ways that will get through to kids.

My goal at the start of this minilesson, in any case, was to be surprising and to draw kids in so they really listened. I wanted to say something that I have said a million times but to say it in ways that made it newly interesting. And I wanted to continue to make book clubs into an exotic, appealing, exclusive sort of a thing. You'll remember that often I've tried to jazz up minilessons by saying to kids, "I have a secret that I want to tell you," and then turning my voice into a whisper. This connection is a takeoff on that. You can see if you think this works or not.

You'll have your own sense of what your kids need. Predictability and structure are important for a while—a long while, I think—but there comes a time when what is needed is unpredictability. You'll need to judge this for yourself.

case something happened in the middle of them, but really, I was skipping over the words.

"But then two things happened to change me. The first is that I was in a book club with a friend of mine, Katherine Bomer. She's a poetic, artsy person. We would get together in our club, and I'd be just about ready to say, 'This was such a boring book. Nothing happened,' when *she'd* say, 'Wasn't this the most exquisite book in the world! Oh my goodness, I kept rereading that one beautiful part over and over, where it described that west wind blowing across the plains and into the open window on the second floor. I felt like I could feel that breeze and the curtains blowing over my face. And then when the moonlight fell on that empty rocking chair—didn't it give you goose bumps? I think that passage was the most important part of the story.'

"To tell you the truth, after my friend said something like that I would be glad I'd never opened my mouth about the book being boring. And after our club was over, I'd go back and look at those passages and think, 'Huh? She thought *this* was important to the story? What'd she see in it?'

"But over time, something happened. I'd be reading a book for our club, and I'd get to one of those slow patches, and I'd be ready to skim past it, and then I'd think, 'Wait. Katherine is gonna love this part. Let me give it a chance.' Then I'd read it, trying to see what Katherine was apt to see in it. I sort of read the passage with Katherine perched on my shoulder. And I'd end up thinking, 'Whoa. This *is* important.' Reading in a club does that to me. I start seeing through the eyes of my club mates.

"The other reason why I stopped skipping those descriptive passages is this. I began reading a ton of historical fiction books. And I came to realize that when I'm reading historical fiction, the descriptive passages are like the parts of mysteries that contain clues—clues to what life was like back then, to what problems the characters are going to face, to how the characters will face those problems."

Name your teaching point. Specifically, tell readers that when the plot slows down in descriptive moments, they have an opportunity to slow down as readers, to soak up details that the author probably inserted so the reader could better imagine this place.

This is a true story, as you can probably tell. Notice that telling the name of my reading friend makes the story feel truer (and by the way, you should read my friend's book for teachers, Writing a Life, *by Katherine Bomer, because it is an all-time favorite). Madeline L'Engle, a marvelous fiction writer, once gave me some advice: "If you want to make your fiction sound totally believable, insert as many concrete details as you can. Instead of saying, 'I looked up and saw elephants flying by,' you can say, 'The oddest thing. I was walking to my car yesterday morning at about 7:10 in the morning and I happened to glance up and you won't believe it—I saw two large pinkish colored elephants fly over me, with a much smaller baby elephant trailing behind. They flew over the park across the street from my house, and out of sight.'" My point, teachers, is that if you decide to tell a true confessions story of your own—insert a few details. It will give your story the ring of truth.*

As I speak, I realize that I am in fact describing a process that could make for a wonderful minilesson sometime down the road, whether in this unit of study or in another: trying out reading like our colleagues read. What a motivating way to lead youngsters into trying new things! I make a mental note of it and plan to jot a physical note to myself when I get a moment. I hope you make these same kinds of notes!

I may be confusing matters by bringing up the comparison with reading mystery books at this point in the minilesson, though I do think the analogy is important. You might decide to delete this reference.

"Sometimes we come to places in a story where there is more description than action. Readers, trust the author. Be loyal, stay side by side, rather than running ahead alone. Probably the author inserted these details so that you could better imagine this place. In good books, readers can trust that we'll learn something important through these descriptive passages. Let's look at one," I said and distributed copies of the opening to Chapter 3.

TEACHING

Read aloud an upcoming descriptive passage, reminding readers to listen for clues to a character's life. In your demonstration, draw on your own life to help you envision, departing from the text, and then let close reading rein you back in.

"Let's start reading Chapter 3 of *Number the Stars*. You can look at the page and see, almost just from the look of the page, that this is not going to be one of those lively, dialogue-filled passages where people are coming and going and talking back and forth. Even from a distance, this looks like one of those slow patches that I used to skip.

"I'm going to remember, though, that when reading historical fiction, descriptive passages often contain clues that help us envision what it is like for the characters to live in the world of the story. So let's read these passages closely, especially noticing details that help us imagine what life is like for the characters. And let's pay attention to the tone, the feeling, of the times.

"Before we read, let's try for a minute to imagine the life. I think the characters live in an apartment building; the Johansens are on the third floor and the Rosens are below them. It is a sunny city neighborhood with people standing in the doorways. Remember that woman watching the girls interact with the soldier? I think the people standing in doorways and on porches are probably standing in the nice sun. There are shops nearby, and two Nazis in their uniforms on every corner.

"Now watch as I read the upcoming page and continue to dream the dream of the story, to feel the mood of it, as readers do."

Chapter 3: Where is Mrs. Hirsch?

The days of September passed, one after the other, much the same. Annemarie and Ellen walked to school together, and home again, always

I imagine I could have said this in a simpler or more familiar form. I am trying to establish the importance not only of envisioning the setting but also of taking cues from authors. Eventually, I will explain that envisionment helps us understand what affects a character. That is, there is a thin line between envisionment and cause and effect. Earlier, in the character unit of study, there was a thin line between envisionment and prediction, and, of course, understanding cause and effect helps one to predict. Once again, you see evidence that reading skills do not exist in isolation, one from another.

I hope I am not giving kids any ideas they didn't already have! That is, I am certainly not aiming to teach kids to bypass these thick paragraphs. But I am pretty sure that a good many children either bypass them or skim them. I hope that positioning myself as a reader in solidarity with those children, and then showing them how to shift from this position, helps.

As you can probably guess, I've deliberately imagined the setting in a way that I will need to revise. It is not warm and sunny in Denmark at the time when this story is set. It is not sunny in the world, and more importantly, no one feels sunny. In my demonstrations, I often show myself deliberately struggling so I can show how I self-correct.

now taking the longer way, avoiding the tall soldier and his partner. Kirsti dawdled just behind them or scampered ahead, never out of their sight.

"I have such a feeling of foreboding. In a way, the book is just telling that the girls do the usual stuff that everyone does, going to and from school, the days passing, but there is a feeling of foreboding about this, of trouble on the horizon. I'm wondering where I get that from. Let me reread." I did, this time underlining key words: "always," "every time," "the longer way," "never out of their sight.

"It's like the girls are *always* aware of the hard stuff that is around them. Think about it. *Every time* the girls walk to or from school, they take the *longer way* to avoid those ever-present soldiers. Kirsti goes a bit behind or ahead of the girls but is *never out of their sight*. And she is the carefree one who supposedly is too young to know what's going on!

"Readers, the interesting thing to note is that paragraph doesn't have too many descriptive details. It's not really describing the place at all, directly, but it does give a feeling for life in that place, doesn't it? No one says it, but it's as though on the surface life is going on as usual, but everyone is uneasy. And yet they're not talking about it. That's the other sense I get. Of fear that is under the surface, not talked about."

Active Involvement

Channel children to listen to the next section of the read-aloud book and to join you in envisioning and thinking about the details of the excerpt.

"Let's read on, and again, let's really notice the tiniest details about the setting—the time, the place—and about the characters' different reactions to it. See if this is the sunny city neighborhood with people standing in the doorways that I pictured. I'm passing out a copy of the upcoming paragraphs. As I read, I want you to annotate the passage. That means mark it up. Underline anything you see that is significant. Look really closely." I read aloud:

> The two mothers still had their "coffee" together in the afternoons. They began to knit mittens as the days grew slightly shorter and the first leaves began to fall from the trees, because another winter was coming. Everyone remembered the last one. There was no fuel now for the homes and apartments in Copenhagen, and the winter nights were terribly cold.

Even if the passage is only in a book that I am holding and the kids cannot see which words I underline, I'll still want to underline. My voice can suggest which words I underline, but the more important thing is that I want to demonstrate the fact that I read very closely, annotating the selected portion of the text, because this is what I am going to ask children to do. You will have nudged kids to refer to the text in their book conversations, but I am taking this a step farther. I do not simply want them to refer in some general fashion to a passage in the book. I want them to actually dissect that passage, noticing the wording itself. Frankly, the first time I read this paragraph I did not see anything much in it worth noting. It takes multiple close reads to mine the sort of details that lie hidden within texts.

Many writers describe the reading that they do by highlighting their connection to the musicality of language. If you taught several minilessons in which you aimed to help children listen to the sounds of a story, reading with an inner voice that brings out the voice of the story, you might tell them about Robert MacNeil, the radio journalist, who wrote in his memoir, Wordstruck *about his experience listening to Dylan Thomas. "I listened as though my whole body were ears. . . . I had never heard such a tumble of wonderful words." He added, "Something began to come together for me that had taken all the time from my childhood to understand: it was the sound of English that moved me as much as the sense, perhaps more" (McPhillips, p. 81).*

Like the other families in their building, the Johansens had opened the old chimney and installed a little stove to use for heat when they could find coal to burn. Mama used it too, sometimes, for cooking, because electricity was rationed now. At night they used candles for light. Sometimes Ellen's father, a teacher, complained in frustration because he couldn't see in the dim light to correct his children's papers.

"Soon we will have to add another blanket to your bed," Mama said one morning as she and Annemarie tidied the bedroom.

"Kirsti and I are lucky to have each other for warmth in the winter," Annemarie said. "Poor Ellen, to have no sisters."

"She will have to snuggle in with her mama and papa when it gets cold," Mama said, smiling.

"Readers, I'm pretty sure you are not picturing sunshine anymore. Earlier this year, we learned that's what happens: We read, we envision, and then we carry those mental pictures with us as we read, and sometimes as we read on and learn more, our initial picture starts to morph. Can you picture those girls walking home? Hold your body in a way that shows how they walk against the winter.

"The soldiers who are always there are troublesome, but life is also becoming troublesome too, isn't it? In your copy of the text, star the exact words that help you realize people are bracing themselves for a really hard winter."

Channel readers to annotate copies of the passage you've read aloud, mining it for hints about the life the characters lived.

I looked over children's shoulders. "Many of you are starring the phrase 'Everyone remembered the last winter.' I hadn't thought of that, but you are right. It must have been tough, if the memory of last winter is on everyone's mind.

"And I'm noticing many of you circled the detail that now there is not even any fuel in the whole city! You are right. The line that says that the Johansens are *lucky* enough to find a couple lumps of coal is pretty amazing. I'm used to lumps of coal being something Santa would put into my stocking if I was bad—not evidence of luck!"

Any time you can incorporate drama into your teaching, do so! Research shows that children (and adults) are more engaged and attached to an event when there is a physical movement attached. Having children quickly turn and act out thrusts them into the scene, placing them into the action, and they are then better able to envision and internalize the scene.

When you say, "Everyone remembered last winter," your intonation is important. Think about what that line really means. Everyone in this city remembered their last winter. Doesn't that make you shiver? There is a grim, ominous feeling to that sentence. You want to show children how easy it is to fly past lines and not really take them in—and how helpful it is to really hear what the text is saying. "Everyone remembered last winter."

Set children up to recall and reenact a time when they experienced something similar to what the characters are experiencing, and then to listen again to the text, empathizing and envisioning. Then ask them to ask themselves, "What am I learning?"

"Right now, can you recall a time in your life when either the electricity went off or you ran out of fuel, or for some other reason it was really cold? Pretend you and the person beside you—someone from your club—are the mothers, having their so-called coffee in that cold place and talking over things. Show me how you'd sit. What are you doing with your hands? Would you glance somewhere at times? What would you see? You are talking. What are you talking about? Right now, start acting the scene out with one person in your book club.

After they did this for a minute, I said, "Listen again to this part of the text, and then I'm going to ask you, 'What are you learning about the characters from picturing this setting, imagining how the people are reacting to the setting?' First, listen up."

> "Soon we will have to add another blanket to your bed," Mama said one morning as she and Annemarie tidied the bedroom.
>
> "Kirsti and I are lucky to have each other for warmth in the winter," Annemarie said. "Poor Ellen, to have no sisters."
>
> "She will have to snuggle in with her mama and papa when it gets cold," Mama said, smiling.
>
> "I remember when Kirsti slept between you and Papa. She was supposed to stay in her crib, but in the middle of the night she would climb out and get in with you," Annemarie said, smoothing the pillows on the bed. Then she hesitated and glanced at her mother, fearful that she had said the wrong thing, the thing that would bring the pained look to her mother's face. The days when little Kirsti slept in Mama and Papa's room were the days when Lise and Annemarie shared this bed.

The children began to crouch together and huddle as if they were crowding together for warmth. Some students began to giggle, but the seriousness of the scene and of the rest of the class quickly diffused the laughter. The students realized that the Johansens' and Rosens' lives were severe, and that it caused people to be more solemn individuals. Incorporating this type of drama helps students go beyond just stepping into their characters' shoes and allows them to really immerse themselves in their characters' situations. It helps to personalize the situation in the text and bring it closer to home.

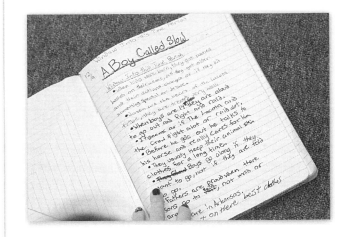

"What are you learning about Annemarie and her parents from the way they are reacting to the setting in this passage? Turn and talk."

Once the room quieted down, I highlighted some of the ideas different students had discussed. "I overheard many of you talking about Annemarie's bedroom and saying that you could almost feel how cold the house was, and you could picture Annemarie and her mother making the bed, spreading the blankets. I overheard Kobe say that the bedroom is a cozy place, but also a sad place because it brought up memories of Lise. I also heard many of you say you could really see the look of concern on Annemarie's face when she mentioned a time when Lise was alive. I even heard Kadija say that she pictured Annemarie stopping making the bed abruptly because she suddenly became so worried she had upset her mother. I even noticed Kadija almost acting that little part out." I showed the students the way Kadija had swept her hand across a make-believe bed as she described this, then stopped, the way Annemarie might have, with a look of worry across her face.

LINK

Reiterate that descriptive passages help readers imagine characters in their settings and feel the tone of those settings. Suggest that readers can help each other see more.

"Readers, I began today's minilesson by confessing that I *used to be* the kind of reader who skipped past the descriptive passages when I read. What I want you to know is that *now* I am the kind of reader who reaches a descriptive passage in my historical fiction book and says, 'This is going to be important.' Sometimes I even read those passages just as we did today, almost annotating them, mentally underlining key words and details, thinking, 'The *author* could have skipped this entirely or written it differently. Instead, the author did it this way. There is probably important stuff here.' I also try to read those sections so that I can almost act out what the characters are seeing and doing. This helps me think about how characters are responding to the changes in their world.

As Annemarie and her mother tidy the bedroom and discuss colder weather on the way, Annemarie remembers a baby Kirsti climbing out of the crib to snuggle in Mama and Papa's bed, which can't help but remind her, and then Mama, of Lise. Because of this small interaction over blankets in a bedroom, we are let in on the fact that Lise and Annemarie shared a bed, which somehow makes her relationship with Annemarie more real (they probably giggled and whispered secrets into the night) and also reveals Lise's loss as being extraordinarily painful. So painful that Mama doesn't like to talk about her or hear about her. If your students seem to have a hard time digging into all of this, you may voice over as they talk, saying, "What memories do the blankets bring up for Annemarie? What do we learn about Mama by paying attention to how Annemarie watches her after mentioning Lise?"

"Today, if you *used to be* the kind of reader who, like me, skipped past descriptive stuff, then I suggest you might start reading time by looking back over a descriptive passage in your book that you and your club mates might already have breezed right past. You'll see that I've duplicated a very small passage from the book that each of your clubs is reading—passages that I think merit close rereading. You may want to start by annotating the passage I have copied, looking incredibly closely at it so you can talk about it when your club meets (and perhaps act it out, too). Very often, the characters are reacting to changes in their world, to events that are happening in that world. If we skip the descriptive passages, we skip the logic that holds the stories together.

"You can get started reading, unless you and your club mates need to take ten seconds to establish a page that will function as your goalpost and to agree on the thinking and writing you'll do in preparation for your club."

Making Our Way Through Historical Fiction

- *Collect setting details. What kind of place is this? What does it feel like?*

- *Is trouble brewing? How is it changing? What feels important?*

- *Collect vital data about characters. Traits? Pressures on them? Problems they face? What drives them?*

- *What new understanding and historical information do you have?*

- *What is the sequence of events in the story, including jumps in time?*

- *Notice what's changing in the book. How are the characters' problems escalating? Has the setting or the mood shifted?*

- *Think about how characters are reacting differently to big events and what we can learn from this.*

You'll probably find it is not all that difficult to skim a book and to locate a passage or two in each book that is worth mining. Look for the big block paragraphs, and skim them to make sure the descriptive details seem to address the major historical conflicts and to show characters' responses. By selecting a passage and duplicating it for children, you remove their tendency to say, "There is no good stuff in this passage!" The confidence that there is gold to mine makes it much more likely that kids will find that gold. And the truth is that almost any passage will yield gold if the reader approaches it trusting that the passage is laden with meaning.

CONFERRING AND SMALL-GROUP WORK

Support Readers' Work with Complex Books

Readers Ground Our Responses in Textual References

"Readers, can I have your eyes and your attention?" I waited. "When you prepare for your clubs today, remember that it helps to bring a passage or two that illustrate your ideas.

"Before you even meet with your club, you'll want to think, 'What *idea* am I bringing to my club?' And think, also, 'What *passage* can I find that captures those ideas?'

"One more thing. Once you've selected a passage, you'll want to reread it really closely before you bring it to your club, like we did in the minilesson today, forcing yourself to try not only to only see more in it but also to feel more, experience more. When I reread the passage in which Mama said to Annemarie, 'Soon we will have to add another blanket to your bed,' and Annemarie answered that she

and her sister were lucky to be able to snuggle together as they slept in their frigid, unheated house, I found myself feeling cold, too, and I wanted to pull a blanket around me. The poet Naomi Nye said that when we read well, we 'may become a lily or pebble . . . for just a minute.' Once you've selected a passaged that illustrates your idea, reread it. Reread it in a way that lets you be bone-cold for a moment. When you and your club get together, you'll want to open your book to a passage that is worth studying and worth experiencing.

"So, you have a few minutes to get ready for your club. Then I'll signal for you to get started."

It had been a few days since I'd checked in with the members of the World War II Club. When they had earlier begun *Autumn Street*, they'd come to me feeling utterly baffled by the first chapter. I'd glanced at the pages that had so confused them then and had been startled by the complexity of the text. I had forgotten that the opening passage seems to come out of nowhere: "It was a long time ago. Though, it seems, sometimes, that most things that matter happened a long time ago . . . by the time it stops hurting enough that you can tell about it, first to yourself, and finally to someone else, more time has passed." The text then abruptly jumps to a whole different image: "If, instead of a pencil, I held a brush in my hand, I would paint the scene: the scene of Autumn Street. Perspective wouldn't matter; it would be distorted and askew, as if through my own eyes when I was six, and Grandfather's house would loom large." On that day, when

the beginning of *Autumn Street* had so confused them, I'd snuck a quick check on the computer to be sure the book actually was labeled a U book—which it is.

I'd pointed out to them then that they were reading a book that was significantly more challenging than anything they'd read before, and that it was typical of the books they'd encounter from now on that often a chapter (especially the first one) would seem to come out of nowhere. I explained that sometimes, rereading a part of a story doesn't help that much until we also read on. "You're *supposed* to be confused by this opening," I said, and reminded them how I'd earlier talked about readers sometimes having one piece of the puzzle that simply doesn't snap into place, and that when this occurs, it helps to just put that one puzzling piece to the side and to read on in hopes that things will become clear. So

I wanted, now, to see whether these readers had managed to get their arms around *Autumn Street*.

Today, as I drew my chair alongside her, Kadija was in the midst of writing a response to Chapter 8. I asked if I could look over her writing as she finished the entry, and she moved her hand a bit to the side so that I could read while she continued down the page. The entry began with the title "Chapter 8: Noah's Death" (I checked the book's table of contents and noted with a smile that the chapters are untitled), and the entry also began with a tiny timeline of the chapter. I noted too, that this was indeed the chapter in which a young boy named Noah, who lived next door to the narrator, Elizabeth, dies of pneumonia. So I scanned the entry, wondering what Kadija's thoughts were about the boy's death. The odd thing was the entry didn't mention the character's death. Instead, Kadija had written repeatedly different variations of one message: "Liz (the narrator and protagonist) did not understand what's happening around her." The entry continued, explaining that the family had kept news of the war from the little girl. Kadija had clearly used prompts that she learned about earlier in the year to extend her thinking, writing such things as, "This makes me think that Liz is out of tune even though she is with a lot of people that know what is going on around them. On the other hand, Jess knows just about as much as Charles does. . . . Liz thinks that she is clueless about these things but it's ok because of her age. She does not care how much she knows."

I asked Kadija if she'd walk me through her thinking about the book, so she showed me earlier efforts to record information on the characters and the setting, all of which described the first two chapters of the book. Since collecting the book's vital statistics, it seemed to me she'd mostly been pursuing a single line of thought: Young Elizabeth was being shielded from a knowledge of the war and was therefore clueless.

I asked Kadija if she'd wait while I did a bit of investigation and quickly scanned Brandon's entries, noting that he, also, seemed to be thinking especially about whether or not the adults should be shielding Elizabeth from a knowledge of the war. I had been hoping that these readers were remaining open to lots of ideas about the story. I wanted them to assume that every detail mattered, and to be going back to earlier parts of the story, even the very beginning, to see how they made sense of more of the details. But instead, I found that they had focused on one idea, and that idea was creating a kind of tunnel vision as they read.

At this point, I was ready to confer, so I gathered the three members of the World War II Club together and told them I'd been studying some of their writing to figure out the talking, thinking, and reading they'd been doing and wanted to hear about it from them. "The last I recall, you were confused about Chapter 1, which seemed to jump from one confusing image to another. Is the book still confusing?"

The children proceeded to explain that they'd sort of figured some of it out and were now on a roll. They'd talked together about how Elizabeth, like Kirsti in *Number the Stars*, was being shielded from a knowledge of the bad stuff that was going on in the world. They were clearly excited by their ideas, and they began talking on top of each other to explain that although parents can think it helps to try protecting kids from the truth, these efforts never work, and kids really can handle the bad stuff.

I needed to teach and move on, so I said to the readers, "The reason I wanted to talk to all three of you is that I can see you did some nice work listing the characters and the setting, and that now you have put that aside and you are reading with the lens of thinking, 'Was it right for the family to try to protect Elizabeth from the war?' Those are both smart things to do: trying to understand who is doing what, what the timeline is, what's going on, and reading to develop a hunch that presumably you talked about. But right now, pat your head." I did this, and they did. I stopped patting my head and rubbed my stomach, asking them to do the same. They did. "Here is the challenge. When you read, you need to do several kinds of thinking at once. Try it. Try patting your head *and* rubbing your stomach."

Try it yourself. It is not easy to do. After a few attempts, the World War II Club and I talked about the fact that to me it seemed that they'd done one kind of thinking as they read the first two chapters, then they'd done an entirely different kind of thinking as they read the more recent chapters, and meanwhile, they'd dropped all attention to following the characters and the main plotline. "I know you have an idea you are growing. It is almost like you are looking through glasses that have 'They're shielding Liz' written on them, but meanwhile you are overlooking everything else. And actually, you are overlooking most of the story. In the chapter you just read, one of the neighbors, a twin, just died, but because it has nothing to do with the idea you are growing, you seem to have sort of read right past it."

I then pointed out that the readers were reading a gigantically complex text, and that most of us in that situation at the start of a book will pause and reread it, expecting things to click into place much more the second time around. The club members agreed to reread the start of the book. "This time," I said, "try to think about the fact that this book shows not just that Elizabeth doesn't understand things. It also shows that she is piecing an understanding together. And the book is written in fragments, in choppy pieces, partly because her understanding of things is choppy; it is fragmented. See if you can continue to try to understand the main things that are going on in Elizabeth's life and the changes in her consciousness. That would be huge. To do that, I think you need to make sure you're not just looking through the lens of one idea. If you keep thinking, 'Yep, she is being kept in the dark, and that's wrong,' you miss out on the fact that this really is a book about how this young girl over time sees more and more of what's going on in the world, including a lot of scary stuff right there in her backyard (not overseas in the war). You'll be trying to understand a child's understanding. And her understanding will be a bit off, a bit childlike, so you're going to have to turn your mind on full blast to understand her dawning sense of the world. I think it would help to go back over the story, even looking right back to the very start, to see if you can include more of the story in your thinking." I left these readers, making a note not to let much time lapse before we met again.

TEACHING SHARE

Readers See More When We Pore Over Passages Together

Ask your students to choose a passage in the book they are reading and then to work together to mine it for new ideas.

"Readers, I want to intervene for just a second as you talk. I love the fact that as I look around, I have seen most clubs pulling close over an excerpt or two from your book. Have you ever been to the ocean and found those little pools in the rocks along the shore? At first those tidal pools seem to just be puddles of water, but if you sit on your haunches and really look closely at them, you see they are teeming with life. You should be finding the same thing when you look closely at the sections of text that you and others have chosen. And remember, because there are a whole bunch of you looking together, you should be able to see things that are invisible to you alone. You should be able to discover things you missed."

"Remember to bring not only four sets of eyes but also four minds to this work. You should be able not only to *see things* you didn't see alone but also to *think ideas* you didn't think alone."

"So right now, go back to a passage (you and your classmates will want to agree on one). Look again. Really look. Pretend you are pulled alongside one of those ocean pools. If at first you find yourself thinking, 'There's nothing that much here,' try looking again. Try thinking again. In fact, pulling close over an excerpt from the text, rereading it, then looking together to discover hidden ideas is another way to grow a powerful club conversation. Let's add that to our chart."

I then began circulating as readers reconvened in their clubs.

Growing Powerful Book Club Conversations

- Be a good listener by leaning in, making eye contact, and letting the person speaking finish his or her thought. You can even jot notes as someone speaks, to honor his or her words.

- Be aware of any member who has gone unheard. Invite him or her in.

- Listen to conversation like it's gold.

- Allow disagreements to generate more thinking. It can help to say, "That may be true, but I see it differently" or "Another way of thinking about that is. . . ."

- Reread an excerpt from the text and look together to discover hidden ideas.

Ask one club to share what they've done and then debrief, naming what they've done that readers can do another time, with another text.

After the clubs had met for about eight minutes, I intervened. Gathering readers' attention, I said, "I want you to hear some of the thinking that people have been doing," and then I gestured for Josh to share what his club had noticed. Because I'd conferred with the Freedom Fighters and was fairly sure that they'd looked closely at a passage from *Roll of Thunder, Hear My Cry* to extrapolate ideas about peoples' lives at that time, I asked if one of them would share what they'd been thinking. Josh surprised me by saying, "Well, we ended up spending half the time in *Freedom Summer*, 'cause after we looked really closely at the first part of the book, we realized that everyone has their own place in the town, kind of. The town thinks that black and white people should be in separate pools, stores, and all, and the town sort of says that to the boys, but the boys kind of go, 'No way.' They stick together because they are friends. They won't swim in separate places or go into separate stores. They stick together and sort of make their own group."

"Wow," I said. "You know what that is making me think? When you described the town, you didn't talk about the *physical* town—like the small houses with big porches, the general store, the creek winding through the fields. You talked about *the beliefs* of the town. That is so amazing—to think we can describe a time and a place by talking not just about the systems of transportation and the clothing but about the beliefs people held. Whoa." Then, speaking to the whole class, I said, "Right now, let's have you and your club pull close not around a passage from your book but around your sense of the place, the setting. Can you think of the setting in your book as a place that has identifiable beliefs? Turn and talk.

Then, intervening in the conversation, I said, "Oh my gosh. I can't get over the ideas that I just heard. Holy moly, when you think together, you are coming up with amazing ideas! Some of you are pointing out that in your book and also in *Freedom Summer*, there is almost like a different setting, with different beliefs, for different groups of people. And you've got me realizing that it is true. What your club helped us to see is that in *Freedom Summer*, it's as if there is one town for the kids, one for the African American adults, and one for the white adults. The town is a different place for different people. And some of you were saying that's the case in your books as well! Wow. And I am realizing—that's probably true of our school, too. This school is a different place for the teachers, for the first graders, for the fifth graders, right?

What a powerful lesson this is—simple, yet vastly important: One's own experience is not everyone's experience. The idea that different characters, and of course different people, can have such hugely different perceptions of and experiences in the same place is yet another way to teach not only understanding and tolerance but empathy. Being able to imagine characters' varied experiences of a place will of course help children imagine the varied experiences of people in their own world, their own setting, which is the first step toward building empathy, and also respect.

"Readers, you're not going to talk in your clubs tomorrow. So take a minute to establish your plan. Because you won't be meeting for a bit, that means it will be especially important for you to write up a storm as you read, so you can save your ideas for two days, until your club does meet. And you have so many things that you could be thinking about and writing about tonight. I'm going to distribute this chart that captures some of the suggestions we have generated so far for the sort of thinking you might be doing as you read, and you'll notice some of this is thinking that especially makes sense at the beginning of a book, and some of it is thinking that makes sense in the middles and ends of books."

Ask readers to join you for a mini-celebration, since you've come to the end of one portion of the unit of study and the work will take a slight turn going forward.

It was time to end the session, and I knew this also marked the end of the first bend in the road of this unit. I asked readers, who had been sitting in small circles with club mates, to gather in the meeting area, bringing their books. I said, "Let's take this moment to celebrate the characters we've come to love and admire so far. When I first read *Exodus*, I wanted to be like Kitty. I wanted to live a life of courage and integrity. I wanted to work with children. I wanted to surround myself with others who were brave. And I wanted to be like her, also, because she learned from her mistakes. She wasn't perfect. In fact, she was really flawed, but still, she was someone I wanted to be more like. She is someone whom I love and admire."

I motioned to the books the children had in front of them. "Readers, take a moment. Think about the stories you have been reading and the characters in these stories. Who do you want to be more like? Who do you admire? Why? Is it Rose Blanche, who gave her life to feed the starving children in the camp behind her town? Is it Monique, who so bravely found her way home when she was separated from her mother? Is it Annemarie, who pledges that all of Denmark must be bodyguard for the Jews? When you have something important to say about a character you love or admire, turn and talk."

They talked. I listened in for a few minutes, then interrupted them. "Readers, I love hearing about the characters you admire, and how you want to be more like them. José wants to live a life of adventure like Bud. He wants to stand up for what he believes in, he said. Brianna wants to try, when she can, to protect those who need protection, like Rose Blanche does.

"Look at this work you are doing! You have given yourselves new role models. You will find yourselves, in unexpected moments, from now on, thinking, 'What would Rose Blanche do?' or 'How could I be more like John Henry?' I'm proud to read with you."

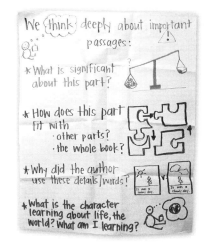

Making Our Way Through Historical Fiction

- *Collect setting details. What kind of place is this? What does it feel like?*

- *Is trouble brewing? How is it changing? What feels important?*

- *Collect vital data about characters. Traits? Pressures on them? Problems they face? What drives them?*

- *What new understanding and historical information do you have?*

- *What is the sequence of events in the story, including jumps in time?*

- *Notice what's changing in the book. How are the characters' problems escalating? Has the setting or the mood shifted?*

- *Think about how characters are reacting differently to big events and what we can learn from this.*

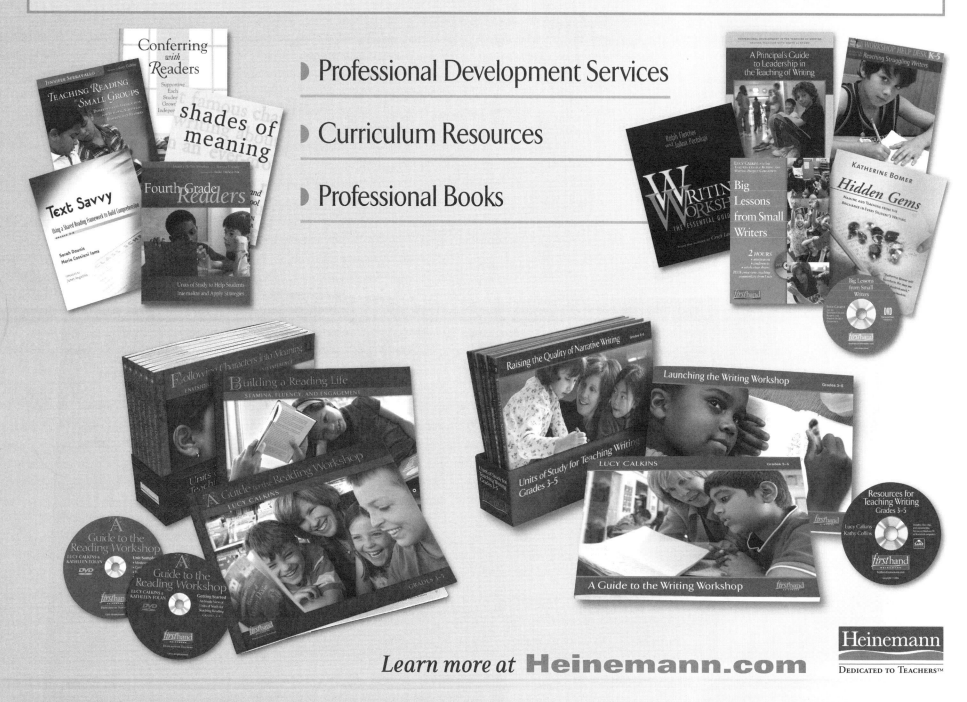

Outfit Your *Reading* and *Writing Workshops* with Proven Resources

▶ Professional Development Services

▶ Curriculum Resources

▶ Professional Books